J M Rowell lives in Norwich, Norfolk, with her partner, Mike, who supports her in her writing. She has always wanted to write a book ever since she was a teenager and if she did not do it now she never would.

Rowell has two lovely children, Natasha and Kelvin, whom she loves dearly. She is also going to be a grandma for the first time.

Rowell works part-time as a check-out girl in *Asda* and she enjoys it immensely as she is a people person and gets to meet some very interesting characters.

J M Rowell

LUCKY LEGS
FIRST STEPS

Olympia Publishers
London

www.olympiapublishers.com
OLYMPIA PAPERBACK EDITION

Copyright © J M Rowell 2014

The right of J M Rowell to be identified as author of
this work has been asserted in accordance with sections 77 and 78 of the
Copyright, Designs and Patents Act 1988.-

All Rights Reserved

No reproduction, copy or transmission of this publication
may be made without written permission.
No paragraph of this publication may be reproduced,
copied or transmitted save with the written permission of the publisher,
or in accordance with the provisions
of the Copyright Act 1956 (as amended).

Any person who commits any unauthorised act in relation to
this publication may be liable to criminal
prosecution and civil claims for damage.

A CIP catalogue record for this title is
available from the British Library.

ISBN: 978-1-84897-406-7

(Olympia Publishers is part of Ashwell Publishing Ltd)

First Published in 2014

Olympia Publishers
60 Cannon Street
London
EC4N 6NP

Printed in Great Britain

To Leslie John Rowell, who was well respected by his friends and well loved by all of his children, by blood or marriage, and to commemorate the passing of fifty years since my mum passed away.

Acknowledgements

Thank you to all my siblings, Christine (Queen B), Rosemary, John, David, Stephen, Robert, James, Jeannette and Lorraine as without you this book would not have been possible.

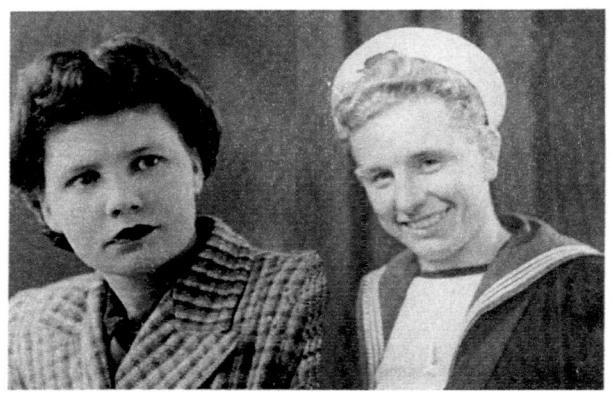

Mum in a checked suit and my dad in his navy uniform

The year I was born, 1953, was a very good year. There was the Coronation of Elizabeth II, although she came to the throne in 1952, and the conquering of Mount Everest by Sir Edmund Hillary. Prime Minister, Winston Churchill, was knighted, scientists identified D.N.A., the Department of Health, Education and Welfare was established. Dr Jonas Salk announced a vaccine to prevent Polio (myelitis) and the successful separation of Siamese twins, to mention but a few events. How lucky was I?

I had arrived into the family of Rowell, consisting, at that time, of my mother, Alice Maud. She had long dark hair rolled into a crown around her head in a war style, as many women did, it wasn't until later that I found out she wore it like that to cover a small bald patch. She was five-foot-eight and I always thought of her as a very attractive woman. She was in the ATS during the war.

My dad was called Leslie John (he liked to be called John, as he said Leslie was a girl's name). He had blond, curly hair and blue eyes; he was short, only five-foot-six, but very much a man. He was in the Navy and, thank God, they both survived the war or there would not be a story to tell. Dad used to box in the Navy, he was volunteered for it by the man in charge saying, 'We are having a boxing championship and I need volunteers, you, you and you.' I think my dad was a bantamweight as he was so slight and he always enjoyed boxing matches. Later on in his life it was a passion he shared with his brother, Dennis. In the war, Dad got a bit of shrapnel in his neck, he had a scar as his war trophy and of course he ended up with tinnitus, that's where you get a ringing in the ears and cannot get rid of it. He got it from working on a submarine with the torpedoes, and the guns on the warships.

Dad always slept with a small radio on his pillow while he slept, so he could not hear the ringing in his ears.

My dad was a staunch Labour man and when he was in his seventies he always said, "I fought for this country and the bloody government has given it away." I know exactly what he meant.

Christine Ann was an after-war baby, born in 1947. She had light hair. Queen B we would call her later in life as she thought we always told her everything, we didn't and still don't of course.

Then there was Rosemary Elsie, a tall, skinny tomboy, who always had short hair. I can never remember it being long.

John Leslie had dark hair like his mum's and a sullen outlook to my way of looking at him. He very rarely smiled and I found him aggressive.

Next in line, David Michael, again dark like Mother, as he got older people called him 'Prussie' and family legend has it that came from gypsy stock. When he was crawling, one of his lungs collapsed, he must have caught a chest virus I suppose. He was left with a weak lung but apart from that, he was OK. This was the family already there when I arrived.

Here I am, Josephine Margaret, small, blonde, curly haired, blue-eyed like my father, his third little princess; he called all the girls that. Oh yes, more to come! Mother was pregnant another four times, not that I could remember seeing her with a big tummy, mind, when you are small you don't always see or take these things in. Later, along came Stephen William, brown haired, a quiet boy, he was eighteen months younger than me, The story of how Stephen got his name, was, that when Mum was seven months pregnant, she got the news of her brother, Stephen's, death. She apparently came down the stairs, hair half rolled, with a pair of Dad's trousers on, got on the bike and cycled up the road to her mother's house on Appleyard Crescent, not too far away, like a woman possessed. She must have been out of her mind because she never left the house without a bit of lipstick on.

Then there was Robert Matthew another brown, curly haired boy followed by twins, Jeannette Evelyn and James Stuart and lastly Lorraine Joan.

When I was just three, I went to nursery at the Dowson School. This school has now been pulled down and has new houses built on it. How Mother ever got me in at that age I will never know, but I can recall that I could read at that age, maybe not well, but I could read, so perhaps that is why. I think I must have gone in the mornings. As I was running down the road one afternoon, after dinner, to meet Grace coming home from work, (she used to live opposite us over on the green), I fell off the curb onto the road and cut my face. She scuffed me up with my face pouring with blood and ran up the road with me to my house. Of course I was howling like a banshee, (not that I knew what a banshee was at that time,)

Yes that's me at the age of three

It didn't half hurt. After that I wasn't allowed to go up the road to meet her, I had to stand inside the gate, or in my case I used to stand on the bar, as I was so short, so I could see her that way. Funny how you latch on to people… I ended up with a big scab on the side of my chin and another under my nose. Vanity must have been with me even at that tender age, as I used to hide under the stairs when anyone came to the door, so they couldn't see what I had done. I have a slight scar on the side of my chin now.

In the meantime, I had obtained another brother, Stephen William, brown haired, a quiet boy, eighteen months younger than me, he said he would soon catch up with me, he does not say that anymore.

Then there was Robert Matthew, another brown, curly haired boy, he had a drip in his ankle when he was born, to change his blood, apparently, he was a blue baby.

I went to a different school, Catton Grove Infants, right next to where my nan lived. She lived on Hunter Road. My nan's name was Elsie Herhoda Rowell (her middle name should have been Rhoda but her father went 'eh' before he said Rhoda and the registrar put it down exactly as he said it). I was always round my nan's, she was wonderful! My dad's mother was so kind and quite short with a comely figure. Her hair always seemed to be in a hairnet, mid-brown fine, (I know this is the exact shade, as this is what I had to ask for at the shops). I liked playing in a seesaw like a boat, with two canvas seats in it. We used to have a sleep (siesta) on little canvas beds and a little blanket. Nan always came to collect me to take me home; I nearly always had tea with her. She seemed to be nearly my mother, which is really no surprise as when I was in my forties, I learnt from Nan's ex neighbour, that my mother, after she had me, took off back to her mum's, leaving my dad with a young baby, so my dad took me to my nan's to look after. Nan apparently said to Mrs Askew, "Look at this little scrap," so I must have bonded with her as a substitute. Mum must have had baby blues, which wasn't talked about then as it is now. Think of all the help she would have had these days…

Apparently it was not the first time that this had happened as when Christine was six and Rosemary was four, John must have been fifteen months, she left to go home to her mum's and Aunt Olive, my dad's sister, offered to look after them. Two bikes transported a double mattress which John sat on, holding the string for dear life, which was tied on the bike that Dad rode, and Uncle John, with his own bike, had the head and foot tied to either side of his crossbar and they all walked up to Earlham, no mean feat for such young children.

I don't know how long they stayed but when they all went back, Mum had come back and she was pregnant again with David, no wonder she wanted some space.

Were condoms about at that time? If so, were they too expensive or was it their choice not to use them?

I loved living in our little three-bedroom house, it was really cosy. Number Three, Soleme Road. The boys were in one bedroom, in two double beds, I can't remember if we had wardrobes. The girls were in the front bedroom, one double bed with one single .I slept in the single, although I always wanted to sleep with Christine and Rosemary. They said I could sleep on the same bed, but I had to sleep across the bottom, on top of the eiderdown so I could keep their feet warm, which like a fool I did.

I used to sit on the inside window ledge, knees bent, reading and I could also watch everyone playing on the green and the houses around it. I loved it; I am still a watcher of people. Mum and Dad would sleep in the other back bedroom with the latest baby in a cot. On the landing stood the chamber pot, talk about a strong mixture, still it cured Rosemary's chilblains when she accidentally put her foot in it. Downstairs, we had the lounge come dining room, a window at each end, a kitchen, and a bathroom that consisted of just a bath and a copper, which was boiled up in the summertime. I used to bathe with my brothers, Robert and Stephen (not a thing that could be done now), we had a bath on a Sunday night, before school the next day, clean vest and knickers (pants for boys) clean stays (I think it would be called a little camisole now), it had little rubber buttons down the front. I know they used to go all dingy in the boil up. Syrup of figs next, if that was not enough, we also had cod liver oil, dished up from enormous bottles. Talk about being regular. There was a back porch with the lavatory, with cut-up squares of newspaper for you know what, and the coal shed. Oh and the pantry at the front of house, near the stairs with the round window Dad kept his bike near the stairs. I've always wanted a house with a round window in it ever since. I haven't achieved that ambition yet.

The garden was more like an allotment; Mother always did the garden. My dad wouldn't, as his father always made his boys do it, rather a bully my granddad was. (Granddad's name was John Rowell. I don't know much about him.)

Apparently, he made his sons take a wheelbarrow and go to the stables to pick up horse manure, bring it back through the streets, and then when they got home, he made them pick out all the straw. His garden used to have prize chrysanthemums and irises. He regularly beat up on my nan and the boys. For some reason, granddad took a dislike to my Uncle Dennis and he was not allowed to eat with the rest of the family – how can men do these things?

When Dennis came home from the Army, his father told him that as he was a man, now he could eat with the rest of them. Dennis refused and ate in the kitchen from that day, until his father died. (Granddad was on medication.) When he had worked, he had been a gym instructor at the Norwich High School. (His father who was my great, great, granddad worked as a gym instructor for the M.O.D.) I don't think he would have been able to work in the schools these days with all the background checks and his bit of a temper. Christine, when she was four, cut half his tongue off with a pair of Nan's scissors, she had to use two hands as she was so small. I don't think Granddad believed that she would, he held his tongue in two fingers for her to do it. She was frightened of him so she just did what he told her to do, as he was a bully as I said before. My mother was told never to bring her round again.

Granddad Rowell died seven months before I was born, committing suicide on Boxing Day 1952 I know I shouldn't speak ill of the dead, I feel as if I am very harsh about him as I had never met him but I was told he even did a performance for that. Nan went to see about dinner and when she went to see where he was, he was standing in front of a mirror, when asked what he was doing the reply was, "I've just taken all these tablets and I want to see what I look like when I'm dying." How sick is that? I suppose his behaviour was because he was a depressive. (I believe that it is now called bi-polar, a much better name, but who knows,) he had tried to take his life several times before, always when people were in the house, so they were used to it. Nan never had a phone, (as many didn't – we take them for granted now) so she had to trot down to the phone box to call for an ambulance. On the way, she met the local police constable (don't you just hate the way police are called

Grandad Rowell – handsome devil was he not?

cops, everywhere in the media and on the television. Such a horrible use of words, I do believe the police call themselves that now) said to her, "What's the matter, Mrs. Rowell?" (the local police knew everyone by name in those days). She told him. He said, "Let me have a look at him." So he went back to the house with her, he called the ambulance but it was too late. I don't think he was much missed by his sons and daughters.

My Aunt June told me another story about this. My father and the other boys would not go for a drink with their dad so he went into a strop, did this thing with the tablets but did get to the hospital. When my dad and Dennis went to the hospital, Granddad told my dad that he could have his new overcoat; the funny thing was that my dad already had it on. But, this story cannot be true or he would not have died through suicide would he? I think it is a story that the boys made up for my Uncle Leonard who was married to June, as he was in Germany at the time and he was younger than they were. They did not want him to know the truth.

Anyway, back to the garden, apple trees, cookers and eaters, pear tree and plums. Mother had a mixture of fruit bushes, then there were the potatoes, peas and cabbages. Although my mum had quite a good food larder, she was an awful cook. I remember the peas that you were supposed to steep soak with a tablet, but she obviously didn't do this as they were as hard as bullets and they would scuttle across the plate. Her batter puddings were always flat, the cabbage was watery but we did still eat it. Her rock cakes were definitely hard! It's no wonder that we were all slim. Sugar sandwiches when we came home from school, now that was a luxury, I don't like them now.

The front grass was cut by Mother, with a sickle or scythe with a wooden handle; she also chopped the wood. She had a black eye once, and everyone thought that Dad had hit her, but she was chopping something that had caster wheels on it, one came off and hit her under the eye with the metal end. Dad would never have hit her.

My mum would stand at the deep white sink (called a butler sink, now what every designer likes) with a cigarette in the corner of her mouth, washing the nappies, (although Christine told me that she didn't smoke but that is what I remember,) with stockings rolled down and a pair of Dad's socks over the top. She would do a boil up on the Monday, well known as a day to do washing, (through all generations of mums). She put a blue bag in, so we had whiter than white sheets and dad's shirts and handkerchiefs then she would take it all into the garden to put through the mangle, an enormous iron thing with wooden rollers. I occasionally used to try to help. I would stand on tiptoe to push the handle up and practically swing on it to get pressure down again, this was no fun in cold weather. Although we did not have much in the way of possessions, we were always clean and patched tidy. Mum would never go out to the shops, or go to Mr. Dean's cart and horse, (the mobile fruit, vegetables and a few groceries store. When I was still very young I saw the horse with five legs. It wasn't till I was about twelve that I realised what it was. The children would know these days wouldn't they?) without putting a bit of red lipstick on. The only colour I could ever remember her using and pulling her stockings up. Must have been where I got my vanity from. When she went out with my dad, she wore a checked brown and white suit, with a brown velvet collar and peep-toe white shoes and a white blouse. I have a photograph of her in these clothes.

Dad worked in the local shoe factory, (Edwards and Holmes, it is now all new homes and the road names consist of jobs in the factory, for example Clickers Row) near Wensum Park, he ended up being the foreman. I can remember he used to bring home old shoe lasts to put on the fire.

Christine can remember he used to mend our shoes with a metal last (we used it as a doorstop in the summer) that had two size shoes on it, tacks in his mouth as he tapped them in. The bottoms of his feet were always pitted and black, I don't know if it was because he stood all day in a glue substance. (I used to love the smell of glue and used to pick the excess off his hands), I don't suppose that we will ever know the answer to that. He did work very hard and used to go in on a Sunday morning so Christine said. Dad and Mum never argued, if they did, the rest of us certainly did not hear them, that old saying, 'not in front of the children'.

Every Sunday morning we, (That was me, Stephen and Robert,) would go to visit Dad's cousin, I don't know why, apart from the fact that they gave us a few coins. We would be dressed up in our Sunday best and shiny shoes. They did not have children of their own.

On Sunday afternoon, we all had to go to Sunday school, John, David Stephen and Robert and I were at St. Catherine's Church. We did get Sunday school outings, I remember going to a great big garden that had a real tree swing on it. I believe that this is when my parents had their quiet time with none of us about? They would always say, "Don't walk on the walls going to and fro from church as you'll scuff your shoes." And of course, who walked on the wall? There was one time that I did and I fell off into one of the gardens. I was that frightened that I wet myself. I cried all the way home with my wet knickers and soppy shoes. My mum went nuts but I didn't get a smack because my nan was there and she said, "If you hit that girl I won't speak to you again." I do believe that Mum did like Nan so she didn't. Nan saved me again. I digress, I was talking about infants' school I don't know why but suddenly I was back at infant school, Dowson School, near where we used to live (I think it's because Nan got a job cleaning at Mrs Neale's, a teacher at the junior school near Nan's.) She was one of the nice teachers. Old but I liked her (old to me.) She lived on Reepham Road in a bungalow. I thought bungalows were quaint then, but I would not live in one now.

I believe her husband was a vicar. We used to have a dance lesson and the dance I liked the most, was the Turkish Delight sequence (that's what I use to call it anyhow). It was a big circle of the girls and boys and for some reason, Colin J always used to be picked as the Sultan. He was quite a handsome lad even then, he had brown, curly hair, lovely teeth and a lovely smile. You are right; he always got me to be his head dancer of the veils. Honestly, fancy teaching seduction to children of that age. Oh yes Colin J was the first boy that I ever kissed on the lips. He lived at the top of Jewson Road, just round the corner into Palmer Road, first house after all the garages. You could see his back garden at the cut-through that was to become Jet Alley. Which was a mucky path that we had made to cut through to the library on Aylsham Road, instead of going all the way round Bullard Road and then Woodcock Road.

Jacqueline S was my best friend at school; we used to go to each other's houses after school. I went to her's more than she came to mine. She had short, tight curls. (Isn't it awful, best friend at that time but can't remember her too well!) I spoke to my friend, Sandra, who used to be friends with Jacqueline's cousin, and was told they were a very quiet family, not very forward, so that's probably why I don't remember her much.

Then came junior school, same place as the infants. Jacqueline was still there and I remember a girl called Josephine M (who would have thought it, two Josephines in the same class) she wasn't always there as she came from the gypsy camp. (Travellers).

I used to have long hair in plaits at that time and I hated it when the nit lady came round to the school, she always undid one plait and never did it back up again. (I think that the mothers of the children take turns at the school checking now.) I don't recall having to have nit stuff on my hair but we probably did. The boys in the desks behind me used to dip the end of my plaits into the inkwell. (The little devils). Now that's what you call a blue rinse. Mum used to get really mad. In the end she cut my hair, didn't put it in rags anymore and Uncle Sam, mum's brother, (black curly hair like a coloured person) didn't seem to like me anymore he used to like long hair on girls or did I imagine it?

This is Uncle Sam. Dark isn't he?

> Sam, Sam the dustbin man,
> Washed his feet in a frying pan,
> Combed his hair with a three legged chair
> Sam, Sam the dustbin man.

This is what we use to sing to him but he took it in good part.

Sam did not talk much, but he talked to Christine, when they went for walks over the Galley Hills, about his war experiences. He worked on the roads, digging holes etc. He married very late in life, when he was in his fifties.

I used to play with a girl called Frances who lived down the road from me. We would play hopscotch on a chalked path with a stone, or play five stones as it was called, all the rage then and if you didn't have the little metal spiders you had to use actual little stones, and another stone to throw up in the air if you didn't have a little ball. I don't recall if she went to the same school as me, but I do know that her dad (or, as I now know it, her stepfather or her mother's boyfriend) used to wear a beret and people called him Popeye. He always used to be nice to us girls, always wanted to have us sitting on his lap. I don't know, but I think he was a bit of a pervert, until you are older you don't realise about these things. His thumbs always seemed to be at the edge of my knickers, rubbing my cheeks but I didn't realise that he was doing anything wrong. As far as I can remember, his hands or thumbs didn't go anywhere else. Can't think what would have happened if Dad had found out.

The whole family always had dinner at home. Christine said Mum always asked her to go down to the shops after she had her dinner and when she came back it would be late, so she would have to run back to school, she used to be sick before she got into the gates, it was all the running on a full stomach. I do think that

Christine was put on a bit by my mum, always doing some little thing for her. I suppose all oldest daughters have that experience, even my daughter used to do things for me and her little brother, the difference is, I did not make her do it like Mum made Christine, although Christine has always been kind-hearted and would do most things for anyone, she still does.

This is Christine holding one of the twins outside in the back garden of 3 Solome road, David in front of her, then Stephen, and Robert in front of him. I was never about when they took photographs.

I can remember dancing round the maypole which was situated in the Dowson senior school yard, that was where Christine used to go, I loved being over that side near her .It was a lovely day when we put on our best dresses and ribbons.

We also danced a few reels. That's country dancing.

Dad often gave Stephen and me a three-penny piece each at lunch times, (weren't we the lucky ones.). I used to love the shape and colour of them (gold colour and shaped like our twenty pence piece). We used to run down to the sweet shop (newsagent's), Blythe's I think, in the crescent of shops on Drayton Road. You could get an awful lot for three pence in those days.

Four chews for a penny, making them a farthing each, (yes they were still about) blackjacks and fruit salad chews, I used to like the multi-coloured sherbet and the sherbet dip with the liquorice to use as the dip, fruit pips and the little sweet raindrop popcorn. Stephen and I once found a half a crown in the hedges on Soleme Road, we thought we were rich (twelve and a half pence of today's money). Stephen does not remember this. I still look in hedges and gutters even now.

As far as I can make out, Mum didn't seem to like Christine much. Was it because she had to marry Dad? (Mum was pregnant) Did it curtail her dreams? All questions which will always be unanswered. Mum's favourite seemed to be Rosemary by all accounts. All us girls had French names. Was it, as I had heard it, that she was in love with a French count or was it all a pipe dream? Did she meet him in wartime?

Joan with Nan Webster

Joan with Granddad

I have no pictures of my mum with her parents.

When Mum was pregnant with Rosemary, they were living with her mother, my nanny (Lily Maud Webster she was the one that looked that dark that Christine said she was a Punjab, I think that's an area of India). I have since started a family tree and I have found out that Grandma was in a home for fatherless daughters of sailors and soldiers in Tooting and her sisters were there with her in 1911. I cannot get any further back than that, as I do not know if Jordan was her father's name or her mother's name. As to why they were put into a home as soon as they were born, I do not know as Lily was in there when she was one.

I can't find any wedding certificate of her marriage to Earnest so we think that they did not marry. Granddad lived in the house too. Christine said he was a lovely man. I don't know how many more lived in Nan's house. I should think Uncle Sam did and Uncle Albert (Brewster), as they were bachelors at that time. Nan said that the two babies could not live in her house, so Mum farmed Christine out to Uncle Stephen (mum's brother) and his wife, Marjorie, they did not have any children so were happy to have her, the only thing was, they lived in London. Stephen worked on the docks, he was a stevedore, and then he went on to the cranes. He was quite highly paid, as it was one of the better jobs on the docks, and one of the most dangerous, later on, he fell right from the very top of the tallest to his death, he was one of the nicest men around so I was told. My dad didn't know my mum had decided to do this and it was done when Dad was at work, when he came home, it was too late. Christine was nine months when she left and she was four when she came back, but they must have moved into the next house by then, which was a prefab (they put them up after the war as a quick housing solution.

There I go again. I was talking about Dad not knowing about Christine going away, Uncle Stephen and Aunt Margery brought Christine home for a visit and when Dad came home from work Mum said, "You've just missed Christine."

Dad said, "Where are they?"

Mum answered, "Catching the train home."

Dad ran all the way down to the train station, actually caught them in time and brought Christine home (this is all Christine's account).

I think he was more upset than Mum ever knew at what she had done.

Aunt Marjorie and Uncle Stephen

Uncle Alan and Aunt Joan

Aunt Joan, my mum's sister, always used to be at our house. I don't think she could have children, she always used to come to Mum's when she was feeling down (it is believed that she must have been another manic depressive as she was always taking overdoses, of course Dad never knew). Aunt Joan was married to Uncle Alan (a mean little man in character). Mind you, they always bought us nice presents.

My Uncle Alan used to work in a department store called Garlands, in the main city, before it burned down and then he went to work in Jarrold's stores.

Mum was always taking in waifs and strays of her family, like her brother, my Uncle Albert, (we called him Brewster still don't know why unless it was because he drank a lot.) as far as I know he never married. He had a cleft palette and when he talked, it sounded as if he talked through his nose. (Like the elephant in Rudyard Kipling's *Jungle Book* stories.)

I must admit I was a bit cruel, as I could impersonate his voice to a tee, but not when Mum was around. He was also the first (Christine said) man to have a cornea transplant in Norwich. Christine went to see him in hospital and it frightened her as he was lying very still, had pads on his eyes and two strainer-like things on top. I suppose it must have looked like a fly's eyes, or how we see them. (The first cornea transplant ever was in 1904).

One snowy Christmas Eve, (sounds like the song) Albert came to the back door, Mum was doing the sausage rolls and mince pies which was the custom in those days, (I kept the tradition when I got married and had children, I have a picture of my daughter cooking with me) anyhow, Mum said, "What do you want?"

Albert said, "I want me greatcoat."

Mum went and got it, he used to leave his stuff at our house. "Where are you sleeping tonight?" Mum knew Dad didn't really want Brewster staying for Christmas.

"I'm going to sleep under a bush over Galley Hill." Then off he went.

Christine said to Mum, "If you don't let him stay I'll never speak to you again."

Mum went out of the back door calling, "Brewster Brewster, come back in, you can stay."

The old devil was hiding under the next door's arch where she couldn't see him.

Mum bought a bed settee, it had two bars like backs on it, which you could take out and put either end like a single bed, again it was to put up her brother Albert.

Again, Dad was not told before she purchased it. (Mum did like her secrets). Christine used to have to meet Uncle Albert to get some of his dole money to pay for his board before he spent it.

Rosemary had a friend, Sandra, who lived the other side of the road, she was an only child. I always thought she was a bit posh (but I met her later on, in a job that I had in an office, where she came to work and she was as down to earth as anyone I know. She is now one of my best friends, not Rosemary's), she went to ballet lessons; she used to teach me what she had learnt, but I couldn't do the tap that she had mastered. Rosemary and Sandra took me to see my first Disney movie, *Cinderella*, I thought it was marvellous I went about singing the songs for ages after that.

I cannot remember that my dad or my mum ever played any games with us as I did with my children. Is it because there was so many of us that they thought we would play amongst ourselves? I used to play Snap with my nan or Beggar My Neighbour (I think that is called Happy Families these days), or solitaire when she was too busy to play with me. When I was around Nan's I used to play with the button box, she had loads and it used to fascinate me, it was one of the things that was handed down to me when she died, as well as a pearl hatpin. She also had a Kelly's Road Directory. It was red; you could see the name of the head of household who paid the rent in it. I used to look for all the aunts and uncles, I still have a curious mind (or like being nosy) about other people lives, as I said, I am trying to put a family tree together now, have got back to 1851 on my dad's side.

We didn't seem to have many toys. When I was four or five, my nan bought me a lovely doll's pram, a metal one, grey body with a navy hood and yes, on Boxing Day my brothers, John and David, thought it would be a good idea to straddle across it and pretend it was a horse, they completely broke it. I was never bought another one in all my childhood. If that was not enough, we girls never seemed to have a whole doll.

Talk about do it yourself, we had a cupboard full of bodies with no arms, legs or heads on them, of course that was the boys again but all Mum said was, 'Boys will be boys'. Does not seem fair to me, why are boys destructive? John and David had their big blue and red tricycles, well they seemed big to me. They had a metal holdall like the boot of a car on them, very posh I thought. They use to let Stephen and I stand on the back of them for our ride, we weren't allowed to sit on them properly. I used to have a toyshop till with pretend money in it, I would use empty packets and bottles as it did not come with groceries as they would now. Oh yes, and we used stones for potatoes as you could get them in all different sizes. I was a very mean shopkeeper, I didn't allow anyone tick as it was called then. (Credit now).

Whenever we asked Mum for anything, her favourite saying was, "When my boat comes in."

Later we would say, "Has your boat come in yet, Mum?"

She would say, "It has sunk at the harbour."

We didn't really know what that meant only that we would not get the thing that we had asked for.

We used to play rounders and cricket on the green, that's where Robert picked up a rusty nail, it went right through his plimsolls. (See his feet again). We all used to wear plimsolls in those days, to play out in as they were the cheapest thing out. (Now they wear them with designer labels, paying a big price for canvas plimsolls that my age group wouldn't be seen dead in now) When it was really hot, we would often sit on the curb and play with the melting tar, we would get a stick and see who could get the biggest lump on it, (the summers did seem to be longer then, maybe it has to do with global warming). In the six weeks' summer holidays (must have done my poor mum's head in) we sometimes went to play on the

Sand/Chalk Hills (I think it's called Galley Hills) and slide down the slopes on bits of cardboard. I wasn't allowed to go but I did use to sneak out. Heaven knows what Mum would have said if she had known that once, I went on the back of one of the T twins' motorbike up and down the hills. They were called Peter and Paul (like the nursery rhyme, two little dickie birds.) Their mother was the local midwife and I thought she was a really nice person.

But, my mother did not get on with her, cannot imagine why not, all them babies she had. She interfered too much for Mum to deal with.

We were often given jam sandwiches and a bottle of water and we went either to Wensum Park, so called because the River Wensum ran right alongside it, (which was next to my dad's workplace). Where, if we could find any swimsuits and a decent towel to take, we could swim in the cordoned off river, I just paddled or sat in it as I could not swim at this time. It was a really strong fence separating the main river, a wonderful idea from the council at that time. (I don't think it's allowed now, all this health and safety rubbish, I think it's because the council don't want people to enjoy something that is free). Children are not allowed to be children anymore (or as free). Mind you, actually going to the park these days seems to be a thing that children cannot do, are there more perverts and bad people about these days? Or do you think that society has made them feel it's alright to do these things? It seems to me that society has gone mad, when a murderer or molester gets fewer years than a bank robber does. (Especially if no one but the banks get hurt). Anyway, I digress again. We would stay on the parks all day playing on swings or hide n seek amongst the lovely gardens, with a bottle of water and loads of jam sandwiches. Waterloo Park, I wonder why it was called that? Was it after the

Battle of Waterloo? I don't think it could have been that, as it was not built until 1933 after the First World War, from government grants, a series of parks that were formal geometrical gardens containing bandstands, pavilions and paddling pools as was Wensum Park. Little did they know that six years later there would be another war playing havoc with all the good things done after the first one. John did not heed Mother's warning about sitting on the gate, as he soon learnt to his cost, mothers do not usually say these things for no reason. Well John was sitting swinging on the gate and he fell off backwards. Ambulance job, his underneath was torn all along his scrotum to his backside as he had fallen on a rough lump of concrete that was there to hold the gate open when necessary. Poor chap he was in the Jenny Lind Hospital for quite a while, and Nan took me up there to see him, it frightened me to see his bottom half all bandaged up. Anyhow I know that us kids used to sing, 'John has only got one ball', (children are cruel) you know the rest. He could still father children, although it would be twice as hard.

Mum would sometimes get a bus to the city on a Saturday afternoon and Dad would line us all up and tell us that we would have to sing to him and if he did not like it, we would have to go to bed. We always used to end up in the bedroom .I think he used to do it to get peace and quiet while Mum was out. We all hoped that she wouldn't stay out too long.

Dad always used to pretend he did not know our names and if he was talking to you he would go through them all except yours and then he would say, 'What is your name?' it would always cause laughter.

We got a television when I was about seven; Robin Hood was one programme that I remember. It came on at Saturday teatime;

there was Muffin the Mule and Lamb Chop, I don't remember too many as I preferred to read.

Well then, what do you think happened? Mum had twins, a boy called James Stewart (after the actor) and a girl called Jeannette Evelyn (middle name after my Aunt Evelyn, dad's youngest sister who died of cancer when she was twenty-one, she also had a twin brother but he died when he was six months old, she had ginger hair always in a ponytail. She used to ride a bicycle all the time). What a surprise for Dad and Mum, (the twins I mean, they did not do all the tests that they do today) another two mouths to feed. They were kept in the back bedroom with Mum and Dad (makes it sound as if they were in prison), they were both given piggy backs to bed most nights and they would giggle like anything although I don't recall that for any of the rest of us. When James was about eighteen months, he went into convulsions, kept rolling his eyes back right into his head. Dad called the doctor, the doctor just said he had a fever with a cold but Dad was not happy with that, so he took James up to the emergency department and found out that James had meningitis,

If my dad had not had the foresight to see that it was just not right, James would probably have been dead or brain damaged. This was a father's intuition not a mother's.

Jeannette was not to be left out of any drama, so being a toddler she had a kettle of hot water over her arm , she has a few red marks on her arm but not deeply scarred from that encounter, lucky, wasn't it?

Just think there were eleven people in a three bedroom house. For the people that say didn't your dad have a television? We didn't until later, when I was older.

Dad would say that he only had to look at my mother and she was pregnant. The time had come to move to a bigger house, council provided of course. It was easier to get on the council housing list in those days or to get a bigger house when needed.

Our new house was on Jewson Road, how splendid, I don't know how we all got there, probably walked, it was not that far from the other house, say maybe twenty minutes if you took all the short cuts, and a shorter walk to Nan's. The house was huge, six bedrooms. It was semi-detached joined by another six bed house and, here's the quirky bit, it had a two bed flat in the middle. Quite clever of the council around that period, the late 1950s. Let me take you through the house that I lived in until I was nearly nineteen. (I have been told by Christine that this little complex has now been made into three, four bedroomed houses). I'll start at the tradesmen's entrance, (back door to you and me). You gained entry by walking down the passageway, which consisted of hedges; I do believe it only had a muck path not concreted and nothing overhead, only a walled arch in between where the walls of the houses began. Our house was on the left side of passage, a little concreted area, step up to the porch. On the left-hand side was the toilet, no change there then, how I hated that toilet and I vowed I would eventually get a toilet that was upstairs, so no one could hear me. To this day I have this thing that I cannot do, you know what now, if I can be heard. In the middle was the back door and on the right hand side was the coal shed. Then into the kitchen, it was bigger than our other kitchen, a horrid green colour on the walls as most kitchens were at that time, big white sink, big wooden draining boards both sides. Mum put curtains in front of them to cover up what was behind .A window looking on to the back garden, not that I could see out (Christine said that this was not clear glass but I would not think that they would only have two top window panes clear.). Talking of Christine, she also says that she used to lock the back door and the door from the kitchen to lounge and would do a strip wash and she would look up at the window and see boys peeping in, John and David used to charge them sixpence a look. (Why did she not take a bowl into the bathroom as I used to when I got older?) There was a pantry with the cold slab, only an air vent in that one, where Christine had seen many a mouse and would scream and jump on a chair. There was a cupboard, which was under the stairs, so it had a sloped ceiling and next to that a bathroom, just a bath, no sink. A door lead to the lounge, which had red lino on the floor and two windows, one at the back and one at the front. There were also two cupboards, one was an airing cupboard next to the fire and the other just an anything (we used it for coats scarves hats etc.). The table was in front of the back window, we must have had enough chairs for us all to sit down at the table but we did have a kitchen table with chairs so perhaps some of us sat in the kitchen. Then there was the door to upstairs and front door, up we go three steps and the window to the right, then a turn up to the rest of the stairs. On the right hand side, at the top of the stairs, was room number one, large with two windows, one looking on to a passageway and the other with the drainpipe near, on to front garden. Room number two was a small room with one window looking onto the back garden and the room opposite, number three, had a water tank in it and a built-in wardrobe. On the left hand side of the stairs was room number four which was quite large with a window looking onto the front garden. Then a long corridor,(like a hotel) and room number five, this was one of the rooms over the top of the flat, two windows, one had like a balcony type thing on it overlooking the flat's garden.

Opposite this was room number six, also over the top of the flat, imagine that in reverse on the other side and we had our own little complex.

The front garden was quite large. It was covered in rose bushes, which as it happens were my mum's favourites, with a hydrangea bush. I love hydrangeas, Mum always put tea leaves on the ground under the bushes and it changed the colour of the flowers. Something to do with the alkaline in the soil. One side of the front door had a slab of concrete attached as a cover from the rain when you went to front door. The back garden door, passage side, round the corner, in front of the kitchen window, had a little flower garden and grass in front of the lounge window where we would keep the rabbit's hutch (I liked rabbits but I did not like cleaning them out much). Then there was a wooden arch, which had dog roses on it, a great long path, again not concreted. On the right hand side were vegetables and on the left hand side, grass, with two apple trees, a pear tree and a couple of bushes that had purple, fluffy flowers like pokers on them and some golden rod. Nan's garden had lots of golden rod near the pond. Then at the back, there were two sheds joined together. John kept pigeons in one side, I hated them. I used to think that they were really dirty (I still don't like them).

Our first night in the new house was very strange; the neighbours made us tea, which I think was a boiled egg and bread and butter. (I will tell of the boy of that house later). Then to bed, the girls were in room number one on mattresses on the floor, as you will recall, we didn't have many beds coming from a three bed house, I can't tell you what room the boys were in. Room number three would be my parents' room. It was the night that I saved my dad's life and I suppose the house.

I laid on the mattress and could not get to sleep as I was so excited at life in a different house, thinking about everything that had happened that day, and then yes, I could smell smoke, not from a cigarette, I smelt that every day (as my dad definitely smoked) but fire smoke. I shouted Christine awake and told her, "I can smell smoke."

"No you can't," she said (she did not want to get up). Then Christine said, "Go to sleep."

"I can't, I can smell smoke!"

Christine said, "I'll go look." (She realised Dad was not upstairs). Mum was fast asleep and did not hear a thing.

Dad had been working all day at the factory and had taken an extra-long dinner break to help men move stuff into a new house. He did not come home from work until ten, people did not take days off just to move in those days .He was really tired and fell asleep with a cigarette in his hand. It fell on to the new mat Mum had bought for the new house, (all these adverts on television were quite correct about smoking late at night). I did not know any of this as I had gone back to sleep and because no one had believed me, we were not to go out of the house. Christine and Rosemary put the fire out with their feet and hands and got little burns to show for it. I found out when I saw his one and a half legged overalls on the line. I easily detect smoke to this day and I do not smoke. (I have tried it but I don't like it.). From then on, we always had a fireguard up as well as making sure that Dad did not fall to sleep with a lighted cigarette.

New house, new school, well not so new as it was the one near Nan but the junior school this time, classes of forty-two children. I believe the most they can have in a class these days is thirty. The headmistress was Miss Thompson, she walked with a walking stick, which she used to put you right, with a little tap of her stick, never really hard, unless you were doing something really bad. A third of a pint of milk we had, I recall orange juice but I don't know when we had it. I think that they stopped it, as it was too expensive. I had real trouble with maths, I was an English lover, drama, geography, and religious instruction was OK and I loved the singing in assembly, it used to cheer me up no end. (I do believe that they are not allowed to sing at assembly because of all the different religions and races now, isn't it a shame, pc running amok as usual). We went home for dinner as it was only ten minutes away and at four o clock we finished for the day, I would often pop in to see Nan.

I used to beg to take the twins out in the pram and yes, we actually did have a twin pram. I was too tiny really but I did get my way now and then, I use to peer round the sides until they got too heavy to push. They used to wear red coats, Jeannette had a red bonnet and they both looked beautiful.

They say new house… yes you're right Mum had another baby. I was told that she was born in the ambulance, in the shop crescent near the lights between Woodcock Road and Aylsham Road, February 1962, Rosemary says that it happened at the phone box on Jewson Road, at the junction between Palmer Road and George Pope Road. Anyhow, it was a ten pound baby, Lorraine Joan, blonde hair, that made five girls and five boys, how's that for a correct balance of nature?

The baby that changed our lives…

*

After having Lorraine, Mum was in and out of hospital, we were only told she wasn't well. Lorraine and I went to stay with my dad's brother, Uncle Joseph, and his wife, Aunt Doreen.

I went to Heartsease Junior School for a while, I didn't like it much, away from all my own school friends. It was a mobile classroom as they had not enough room inside for all the children that went there. Lorraine slept in a drawer and she was always crying, so Doreen said I slept in a room with my cousin, Teresa. Let me describe their house. It was very nice, you went in the front door to a long corridor, on the right hand side was a wall, made half of a reed effect glass, very posh. A door on the right led to the lounge, it had a piano in it. My Uncle Joe could play, I used to love hearing him play what I called honky-tonk music, like Russ Conway who used to be in the charts. He had a radiogram, which had a record player in it. He had the *Robin Hood* record and *The Little White Bull*, I especially liked Robin Hood. Joseph's son, John, learnt to play the piano and he could play a mean classic. Then came the stairs, then a door into the kitchen which was an L shape, you could also see through to the stairs as it had the same reed effect glass down the side. It had three bedrooms and a bath with toilet upstairs (that was heaven for me.)

Doreen couldn't cope with Lorraine's constant crying and had to send her home. Don't know when Mum came home but she was in bed for most of the time.

We used to have to go into her room before we left for school and when we got back, so she could see that we were safe.

The one time I was late coming home from school, (I went around to a friend's, not many of my friends came to mine). I didn't half get a telling off and had to promise never to be as thoughtless again. Mum and Dad still slept together, even though she was ill.

Mum had a hole in her stomach, she used to have to have sellotape over it, as Mum was allergic to the plasters, it was the rubber in them (I found out that I was allergic to rubber many years on). Christine was put upon as usual, she did work hard to keep things going. My ninth birthday came, I got quite a bit of money and I went and bought loads of fruit for my mother. I don't think Mum could actually could eat it, as she was fading fast (although I did not know it), but I'm sure my brother Stephen who, when he was not at school, was beside her bed, ate most of it. (Stephen was a funny kettle of fish you would think that he was her only child but he was for sure my mother's boy.)

Aunt Joan had bought me a lovely metal tambourine for my birthday and the boys took me on Waterloo Park with them, as I was officially old enough to be seen out with them after five o'clock. I played my tambourine on the way, it made a lovely sound. When we got there we went on the swing park and in the shelter, there was an older boy who asked me, "Can I have a go on your tambourine?"

I said, "I only got it new today, for my birthday."

"I'll give you sixpence if you let me," he said,

"Give me the sixpence first." So he did. I ran off to play on the slides, they were in three sizes, made of wood, I went on the biggest. I only had a dress and knickers on, and guess what? I got shivers in my bum (They call them splinters). I got them because someone had started picking at the wood with a knife and left it all rough. I cried and shouted to the boys and they said, "It's a good job you went on the big one as on the middle one someone has put razor blades in between the boards." What a sick, sadistic mind that person must have had. Anyhow, I ran to get my tambourine and ran home.

Christine was there when I got home and I had to lie across her lap so she could get the shivers out. I made her lock the back door so no one could come in and see my bum in the air. "Stop being a baby," she said. She never did like me snivelling but would you have done? She was getting them out with tweezers but the bits that were left she got out with a needlepoint. OUCH!

Christine was talking to me the other day, about the incident that happened between Stephen and her. Mum was in hospital and Stephen had made her a clay tiger, brought it home, he was about seven at the time. Christine picked it up and asked what it was meant to be? He said, "It's a tiger."

She said, "What this old thing?" (To this day, there is a dispute about whether she actually bit the head off or she just pretended and the head fell off because the paint was still wet). Well, apparently, the next thing she knew, he ran at her, chased her up the garden path and took hold of the first thing that came to hand (the garden fork) and threw it with all his might. It's a good job that Christine was a decent runner, she had reached the shed door and got in right quick as the fork hit the shed door and the prongs went straight through it. (What force for a seven year old in temper). As usual, I was not there, (round my nan's). I missed all the excitement.

Dad always called him tiger after that event.

The doctor was always calling at the house and it was overheard that he said to Dad, "Alice is a good woman and I would give my left arm to be able to save her." They could do nothing at the hospital to save her.

Twenty days after my birthday, my mother died.

The night before she died, she sent Christine running about the street to find a shop that was open as she wanted some honey and borax for her dry throat. I have never heard of this but of course, no shops were open then not like they would be today. She shouted at Christine that she hadn't tried. "I've had enough. We can hear you are getting better," Christine shouted back as she slammed the door shut. She leant on the door and said to herself,"You're not are you."

That night, Dad took John and David out with him to give Christine a rest, as she was as stressed out as anyone could be. After Mum died, the rumour got about that he was out getting drunk instead of being at home to look after his wife, we all know where that rumour came from but I shall not say. How could he be getting drunk with two children in tow? I have only ever seen my Dad drunk twice and both times he was in his sixties.

Mum must have died in the early morning as apparently Dad got Rose up early to tell her before he told Christine. She got a comic to read while Dad told Christine, she in her haste had put her dress on back to front thinking she was about to get told off for some little thing.

Dad told her that Mum had died and she said, "How do you know?"

"How do I know?" Dad said, "I surmise that she is." (Christine has hated that word ever since).

Christine then ran into the kitchen and the bathroom and turned on all the taps. I think it was to drown out Dad talking, as I think that she thought, that if she could not hear him then it was not true. She ran back into the lounge then back into the kitchen and bathroom and turned them all off. She ran back into the lounge where Dad caught hold of her and I think he slapped her to calm her down and told her to sit down while he went to get Nan.

In the morning, we were told not to go up to say goodbye as we were leaving for school. It was then that we were told Mum had passed away in the night and was now out of any pain that she had had. (I think not being allowed to say goodbye to my mum has made me fear death ever since).

Stephen, years later, told me that he snuck upstairs to see Mum and he told me that she looked quite peaceful; it was very brave of him to do this.

I remember that I was only nine and when I went to bed on the eve of her death, I went in to kiss her goodnight as usual and instead of saying goodnight she said 'Goodbye'.

I didn't think much of it at the time, but why did she say goodbye? Did she know she was leaving us that night? Who knows?

Dad still slept with Mum, with a bolster down the middle so he did not roll on to her but would be there if she needed him, and also all the all the other rooms were full of us.

No counselling for children in those days!

I do believe that my brother Stephen could have done with it and I still do.

Then we were packed off to school, the most awful day of my young life and we still had to go. I fell off a chair at school and a form in the hall. I don't know why, perhaps I had all that emotion inside and that falling off brought tears to release it. (Who knows?) When it was playtime, my teacher, Miss Churchill, asked me what the matter was. I said "My mum has just died," and she said, "Why did you not tell me?" Then she pulled me into her arms and gave me a big cuddle while I cried over her pretty clothes (she was a very beautiful woman and had red hair and eventually went off to Toronto to get married). She took me to the headmistress's office and I stayed there until school ended.

The day of the funeral was just as bad; we had to go to school, not allowed to go to the funeral, not like the young ones today. Did not have the right clothes anyhow. After school, Dad had arranged for us to stay with Mrs Thompson (headmistress), we went over to the nursery, had some squash and biscuits, I suppose that was a nice gesture (all the women fancied my dad as I was to find out later). So, that was the end of my somewhat idyllic childhood because although I was only nine. I now had to grow up fast.

Rosemary, Josephine, David, John, Christine
Robert, Jeannette, James, Stephen, Lorrainne

A picture I was at home for. Must be after Mum had died.

My poor sister, Lorraine, has never known her mother, the twins knew her only for a short time but they have no memories of her, and for myself, I only have a few. Many years later I found out that Mum died of cancer of the womb and she also had thrombosis, it was two months before her thirty-ninth birthday, there was apparently her and one other lady in Norwich that were the only cases around at that time .Did they find out after she had had Lorraine? (Was it all the babies she had that had kicked it off?). Or did she have it before Lorraine was even conceived? My dad was a year younger than Mum, just think, thirty-seven and a widower with a family of ten to feed, clothe and nurture. When Dad went to sign on, he was told he couldn't because his circumstances were not relevant, as he had made himself jobless to look after us (he would have got no end of help now so he could keep us all together).

Christine holding Lorraine Uncle Alan
Holding the twins in the back garden of Jewson road

I have no mementos of my mum, she did not have a lot of jewellery, the only thing I ever remember is a necklace, a chain with diamond-looking stones, I think, that lay broken in a drawer. I have a picture of her and that is all of her that I have. She is in her checked coat and it is a photograph from the newspaper in her ATS group, although it's very hard to see which one is of her.

When Christine looked through Mum's things, she found that Mum had kept some crayoned drawings that she had sent from London when she had been living with Uncle Stephen and Aunt Marjorie but she threw them out, so Mum must have cared about her really.

Christine told me that Mum and Joan used to share the checked suit. It was brown and white with a brown velvet collar, as they were both up and down with their weight, although Mum could not wear the brown shoes that went with it as she had bigger feet than Joan who was a size 3/4 just like me. My sister, Christine, keeps telling me that I have got her feet, short and stumpy. Talking about stumpy, my son said to me the other day that he had found a way to remember my house key it's short and stumpy like me (blooming cheek)…

My dad used to be a bookie's runner and when he went to see the person he did it for, Dad said, "I don't know if you know but my Alice has died."

The bookie said, "I knew your Alice well as she did a bit of running for me." Something else she kept secret from him .It was her pocket money.

Just after Mum died, we had some Jehovah's Witness come to the door. Dad was working nights, he had seen us off to school and then gone to bed, so I don't suppose he was in a good mood when they came knocking. (I am not against anyone's religious beliefs but why do they tout on peoples' doorsteps and make their children do the same? If people wanted to be a Jehovah's Witness, they would seek it out for themselves). Dad said, "What has Jehovah ever done for me, he has just taken my children's mother away from them how good is that?"

They said, "Sorry to disturb you in your grief."

Dad went back to bed and when he got up later there was a box of essentials on the doorstep. Sugar, butter, tea, bread and milk. I know Dad always said a kind word to them when he saw them out and about.

Dad had a friend who we used to call Uncle Alfie, but he was not a relative. He would always wake my dad up about twelve o clock .He didn't seem to get the concept that my dad had to sleep as he was on nights. I don't suppose that my dad would tell him not to come round. They used to go to the pub for a dinnertime drink. *The Prospect* on Penn Groove, off Aylsham Road. (Which is now a Doctor's Surgery). I had my first taste of Coca-Cola from there, as most children know, many of us used to go sit outside of pubs when we were younger, waiting for parents. Dad went in, brought out a big glass bottle and I sat down on the bench to drink it. I found, to my surprise, that I did not like this drink that everyone was raving about. What did I do? I tipped it down the drain so Dad thought I liked it. He came out asked if I wanted another. "No thanks that was more than enough." We were, believe it or not, quite polite children, it was how we were brought up, to respect our elders. Not like now when you even hear four-year-olds swearing, and teenagers are so aggressive. Then on to the *White Cottage* (which has now pulled down), it was practically next door to *The Prospect*, it used to have a cut-through to get to Waterloo Close onto the park.

All the old bombed houses that were in Philadelphia Lane weren't pulled down until the late fifties. I saw this transformation take place while there were still people living in the ones that are now Sleaford Green area. (Shirley H, another school friend used to live in Sleaford Green with her family, in a very small terraced house). The houses were put up in the sixties. They were built a bit like prefabs, as I remember seeing the made up walls, so they went up fairly quickly. The lane was split into two, the top end was called Penn Grove and the bottom end, Philadelphia Lane. My dad's favourite pub was *The Windmill* on Aylsham Road. To this day, I believe this is where our inheritance went (that's what all the family used to laugh about when we were older).

Uncle Alfie, (not our real uncle but we had to call him that for respect), used to pick him up in his Jaguar, very posh at that particular time, he was retired (or his own boss) and could do what he liked time-wise. (I don't know what his job was but he always had plenty of money). Dad used to walk back to get our tea ready, which was usually sandwiches, as we used to have free school dinners now. How I used to hate the degrading tickets that we used to have that said free on them, as children are cruel, no doubt about it.

Dad used to go and have dinner at Nan's Tuesday and Thursday, meat patty or her delicious mutton stew, steamed puddings (makes your mouth just water, as unlike my mum, my nan could cook). When we all went out to work, Dad paid Nan to make a patty for all of us on a Tuesday. Stephen apparently told his wife never to make this for him after they got married. Life was in turmoil, no one to wash our linen, well most of it anyhow. Nan took to washing dad's shirts, handkerchiefs, pants and vests and she also did mine so I suppose that was pretty unfair of her really but of course I did not mind. Stephen and I went to the laundrette (he does not remember it) one Saturday and caused absolute chaos. We put too much powder into the washing machine and yes, you're right, bubbles everywhere just like you see on the television, we couldn't stop them. We ran off so no one knew (it was empty when we went in) it was us and we went back later to pick the washing up when the bubbles had died down. We put it all in the bags to bring home to put on the line. (Didn't use dryers as that was more money). So we had to bring it all home, it was heavier than when we took it, and hung it on the line to dry. I mean me, as Stephen would have thought his task was at an end when we brought it home.

Dad bought a twin tub with mum's insurance policy so we didn't have to go to laundrette again, and Christine's poor hands would not be red raw and cracked from the Tide powder when she had had to wash by hand.

Christine came home one day to see Dad sitting next to a man with a clipboard, Dad had apparently got behind with the rent because he could not go to work as they said he had to have someone at home and they had come to see what they could sell to pay off the arrears. They said that we could sell the washing machine. Christine went ballistic.

"That washing machine was bought with my mother's insurance money for us ten children so we haven't fucking got anything to sell so you can piss off."

Never has a man moved so quickly from the house.

After he had gone, Christine, who you may remember had turned fifteen that August 1st and was a lightweight, turned round to see Dad, head in hands with his shoulders going up and down, she thought he was crying, but he was laughing like anything.

"You sure can go when you get your dander up girl."

"They said we were well off because we had it and they wanted to take it away."

For all the aunts and uncles that we had, I don't think any of them did anything to help the family. I know that seems a bit harsh and they all had their own families, but I cannot remember one of them coming round to help us with any housework or cook a dinner. Was it because they thought that Aunt Joan was being paid to do it and they did not want to interfere? All they had to do was to ask us, I'm sure that we could have told them that the only thing that she did was to crack the whip at us to do the work. My dad's mum was the only person that helped out.

We had to do chores now and the best one was cleaning the red lino in the lounge. All the furniture that could be, was taken out and put in the kitchen, then the lino was washed and polish that came from a tin was put on it, then we would put rags (dusters to you who could afford them) on our feet and used to slide up and down shining it, all great fun. All in all, we did an excellent job. We still had the rug with the burn in it. This is where my hatred for housework comes from. Worst of all was changing beds and making do with the sheets that we had. Quite pitiful really, we either put the top to the bottom and a clean one on top, or just turn it around so the bit where our bodies had been was on the reverse side. I believe I must have had a dust allergy as whenever I did brisk stair cleaning or doing the beds. I used to sneeze; my eyes itched and blew up like golf balls. Family used to say that I did it on purpose just to get out of doing anything in the house, as I said I am a very girly girl. Still you had to think that you were better off than some families as we were never dirty and I liked to think that we did not smell.

Lorraine was still always crying, I remember one Sunday morning she had started to cry again, (do you think that she was aware of all the turmoil around her she must have sensed something even at that early age?) I got her in bed with me and God knows what happened (remember I was only nine at the time) but she fell on the floor, so what did I do before anyone came up to investigate? I quickly put her in the bed (she did not fall on her head thank goodness) and got on the floor myself and told Christine that I had just fell out of bed.

The twins, James and Jeannette, went to live with Aunt Joan and Uncle Alan, so did Lorraine, good of them, or so we thought. (It was my mother's last wish apparently, that Lorraine be adopted by Aunt Joan). They lived in the next road that went off ours so we could see them when we wanted. I don't know how long the adoption took to go through. (Dad would never have let her adopt her if he knew then that Joan had a mental problem). As we got older, Dad said it was the worst thing that he had ever done, Mum's dying wish or not. This year Mum has been dead for fifty years. We have just celebrated Lorraine's fiftieth birthday and at that party, Lorraine's daughter, Rachael, was talking to Christine, telling her that her Mum actually still feels like an outsider to the family although we have always tried to include her in everything. I listened and I learnt that when Mother was having the twins, although she did not know it at the time, she was going to give the baby to Aunt Joan but as she had twins, she did not want to separate them. So I suppose she was going to give Lorraine to Joan anyhow, but she would have been there to keep an eye on her as she must have known how unstable she was. I do not know if my dad knew of this plan of hers but I can't believe that my dad would have given any one of us up unless Mother had died.

Aunt Joan did not want Lorraine to know that she had brothers and sisters, (I think this was a sign of her instability) and tried to keep her as far apart as she could, even moving later on so we could not be near her, but we always sent her a birthday card to sister not cousin. There was no way that they could stop us. Aunt Joan use to rip them up and Lorraine would not see them. I do believe that Dad made his peace with Lorraine before he passed away. When

James, Lorrainne, Jeannette

Lorraine's first teeth came in, they came in bad, was this to do with when she was in the womb? I cannot remember any other family member having this problem. Robert had great big front teeth but not quite rabbit-like. James and Jeannette had a nice life so we thought, but James was cruelly treated by Uncle Alan, always getting smacked or pulled along by his ear for some silly reason, making noise Jeannette told me, it was aeroplane noises ,or messing his clothes up, I think that they only wanted the girls. Well Rosemary saw this, when James told her what was going on when he was crying, she went round the corner and brought them both home. Dad must have got a shock to find them home, he must have agreed with it, as they did not go back to living around the corner. A bit of Deja vous. Christine all over again apart from the fact she was not badly treated.

James and Lorraine

Jeannette and James   Joan, Lorraine, Robert
                             James and Jeannette

Joan with one of the twins, Stephen and Robert.

Dad got a job working nights at British Road Line and Christine and Rosemary were to look after us. Like that, Dad would be there in the mornings and when we came home from school. There was talk of the girls being put into homes but my dad fought against it as it would be splitting us all up. (It was because, I do believe, of all the incest and abuse that seemed to be prevalent in that era). I couldn't understand when I was a teenager why my dad would get so angry when we used to walk about in our underwear or left menstruation things about (Lillets/Tampax or towels), in a bag on the fireplace so we could pick them up when we went to the outside toilet), where the boys could see them. I now know of his concern to protect us all. He or the boys would never have harmed any of his princesses in that way.

*

They say that life goes on, it does but it can be very hard and traumatic. I often wonder what sort of person I would have turned out to be had Mum lived.

I still went to school at Catton Grove and the headmistress was still Mrs Thompson. While I was in that school I constantly got nosebleeds that lasted a very long time. I don't know the reason why, the old key trick never did any good nor pinching my nose hanging my head over the sink. So I used to end up going round Nan's. I never had many clothes but Nan seemed to know quite a few people and I had new dresses by way of a family from around the corner on Palmer Road. I remember a girl called Jeanette M living in the same house but they were not her clothes as she was quite a bit taller and more robust .I think that they were from a girl called Sandra Y. I always had big hems on my clothes and she always told people that I had her cast-offs on, as I said before, children can be cruel.

Dad bought a set of barber's clippers and scissors so he could cut the boy's hair himself, he lent them to my mother's brother, Uncle Russell, and he never got them back. The boys had to go to his to have a haircut and he did literally put a pudding basin on them and cut round it. If I had not seen this done with my very own eyes, I would not have believed it.

Uncle Russell, he was a legend, the police stopped him in his old van one day for speeding or something like (he always had an old something in his garden, doing it up etc.). Apparently, he put a curse on the policeman, he had an old wishbone in his van. Everyone called him Wishbone Webster after that.

Russell was the most gypsy-like of my mum's brothers that I knew, we did have another of Mum's brothers that used to travel with the fair, but I did not know him. Apparently, *The Eastern Daily Press* used to do pieces on the fairground people and Dad got the reporter who did it, to get in touch with him, to tell him about his sister Alice. I believe they used to call him 'Darkie' because, as I said before, Grandma was very dark and it had come out in most of her sons.

Aunt Margery was his wife. When we used to go around for a tea party, (I hated going round theirs as they always had dogs around so the yard smelt and there was always dog hairs in the food) she made very watery custard, but I suppose it was because there was so many of us. Margery was a very kind-hearted person.

Nan used to take me most places with her at the weekends. I was very lucky in that way I suppose, many times I had to get off the bus because I had travel sickness (still get it today if I sit in the back of a car first thing in the morning), Christine told me she had the same problem.

Uncle Russell and Margery's wedding day

My Aunt June, (my dad used to like her best of all his sister-in-laws as she was such good fun, very dark hair like my mum's) and Uncle Leonard (my dad's brother, he worked on the big telephone derricks, he went all over the place, a very handsome man) were some of the people Nan took me to see. They lived up on the Heartsease Estate, Chipperfield Road, in a very new looking house. It was a three bedroomed house, it had an inside passage that went from the front door to the back, the floor was made of concrete, so you could use it like an utility room to put bikes and outside toys in. Aunt June was quite a good dressmaker and she made me a pink dress with box pleats in it. I wore it to enter a twisting competition at the hospital fete, there was a proper DJ and I think he used to be resident at the Samson and Hercules at that time, it was all very exciting, I didn't win but it was fun. I won a skipping competition though. The dress was used as my party dress, not that I went partying much.

Another aunt that I used to visit with Nan, was Aunt Olive (my dad's oldest sister) and she was a bit religious but a very knowledgeable person who talked very quietly and knew lots about every subject and my Uncle John (he worked as a hospital security person and he was an ex-army officer). He was a very scary person and very strict. I was quite scared of him, I am inclined to believe that he was very much like my grandfather (they do say that girls go for men like their fathers). They lived in Wycliffe Road, North Park Avenue, near Eaton Park (another park built after the First World War. Another one built on the geometric design). All his children are very brainy types and have all got on very well in the world. One thing that I do remember of my Aunt Olive, is that she had a lovely singing voice, and her weak tea. My nan and I used to laugh about the tea on the way home. I had another wall incident at Aunt Olive's, walking on it, lost my footing and made a deep cut in my leg, still got a scar from that.

*

The last teacher I had in Catton Groove School was called Mr Simpson, I think he was a very strict teacher; we never got away with anything. We always had ten words to take home and learn on the Monday, we would have a test on the Friday and if you got any wrong, you would get that amount of whacks with his big white plimsoll, (he would not be allowed to do that now and I did not think it was a necessary practice). We also had to write out any spellings that we got wrong in our exercise books ten times, the teacher would have put the correct spelling when he/she marked books. This is why I am a pretty good speller these days (Or so I like to think). They do not do this when they mark books now that is why the generation in their thirties downwards cannot spell. I went to my daughter's parents' evening at the Heartsease School (called Heartsease Academy now, we are getting more and more American) and told the English teacher that my daughter was an appalling speller and he said, "She can use a dictionary."

I said, "How can she if she does not know, maybe the second and third letter of word?"

He gave me no reply. My daughter still can't spell very well. Although she reads very well, like me she could read at an early age.

On sports days, we never had anyone come to watch us, not that I was very good at them. At hurdles, I had a good technique but no speed, even though I was short I could jump very well. I also used to throw a mean javelin; I liked doing that, as it was a bit more aggressive, a very good way to vent a fury.

If I was just running, my knee would give way and I used to fall over so if I was in a relay team, my team never won. The girl that I remember most for sports, was a girl called Jill C, I have never seen a woman or girl sweat so much when running, it ran in rivulets down her face but she was incredibly fast.

I learnt to swim in my last year at Catton Grove. Mr. Simpson took us; we had to walk up to St. Augustine swimming pool. It was a new pool in the sixties, and very nice at that time, (my dad, in the summer, used to go to the baths there. He paid his shilling and took his own soap and towel, as in the summer we would not have a fire and that is where the hot water came from in the back burner, we used the copper) anyway, I did not like the water, it took me a long time to get into it, even in the shallow end. I was not very tall at ten. I was only four feet nine inches when I left school at fifteen. Dear

Mr Simpson pushed me into the water, I thought I was drowning and to this day I do not like my head under water at swimming pools. I did eventually get my ten-yard certificate, (really twelve and half). It was the only one I ever got for swimming.

David went to that school with me for a little while, then he went to Norman School. I don't know why. I know that he went into special reading classes. James also had a problem with his reading.

Stephen P was in my class, he is now a dental surgeon (I know because when I had my wisdom teeth out at Wayland Hospital, I had the stitches out at West Norwich Hospital and he was the dentist that took them out, how embarrassed was I).

Kevin W, (I had a fancy for him) is now an auditor (I know this as I met him in a workplace that I was at). These two boys were the brainiest in the class; they were always at the top of the chess ladder. I was always one or two from bottom. I can give someone a game but I am still not good. (I taught my son to play he used to be very good at it).

*

We never got Easter eggs after Mum died, we used to get really good ones but dads never think of things like that, plus, he could not afford it. Christmas was always a bit sparse as well. Board game compilations (Ludo, Snakes and Ladders, Tiddlywinks and Draughts), a packet of cards, mostly we got clothes, a new pair of pyjamas, a jumper maybe, a pair of slippers if we were lucky. Aunt Joan use to buy us a stocking with chocolates. Nan always bought new handkerchiefs for all of us. "You can't have too many," she would say, they were quite expensive in those days. I probably should not say, but I have known her to pick them up in the street, take them home, give them a good old boil up starch and iron, good as new yes, and sometimes a book as well. (I always got a book, she knew I just loved reading, *Heidi* was one book and *The Hobbit* was another. (I cannot understand why they didn't make a film of *The Hobbit* first and then the *Lord of the Rings*).

Dad did used to buy a crate of pop (Corona) for Christmas, two orangeade, two soda cream, (this was my favourite it tasted like ice cream) two limes, two raspberry, two lemonade and two dandelion and burdock. This is the only time that we had pop in the house. I think Nan made mince pies, I don't think that Christine made them, and a Christmas cake from the baker's van, pre-ordered. I suppose we had a turkey and the usual trimmings. The tree was always a small, real one, about three/four foot.

Did artificial ones exist then? The tree smell was nice. Icicles, which were just meat skewers, cotton wool for snow, a long garland with shaped glass beads on it, (this was my mum's favourite), we didn't have single baubles that I remember and the sugar mice that had no heads on, as they always got bitten off, (I know I did not do it). We did have ceiling garlands, which were getting a bit tatty and we always made newspaper chains, bit of gum and a lick was all that was required.

Dad worked for the B.R.S. night times, which was a haulage company (I think it is called Lynx now if it still exists). At Christmas they used to have a party, usually at the T.A. centre on Aylsham Road and I think four of us used to go, John, David, me and Stephen.

Dad used to say, "Eat as much as you can, you don't know when you'll eat the next meal." You couldn't eat what you liked anyhow, as you all had a plate made up for you so everything was shared properly. They used to show a film as well, so it was quite good.

Uncle Alan (Joan's husband) used to come round at night to make sure the boys were in bed, he was such a weird little man. I would like to know what sort of man would sit on the stairs and wait for children to make one little noise, even just talking, and then give them a smack. We were children for goodness sake.

After Mum died, I suddenly started to have bronchitis, about every six months, I cannot remember having it before. It wasn't quite so bad in the summer, winter time I would cough all the time and I would to sit up in a big chair downstairs so as not to disturb everyone else with their sleep. The boys used to bank the fire up (talking of banking up fires, Dad used to tell us not to use too much coal, so we tried not to, but Dad still kept moaning about it and one morning he caught the next-door neighbour, the father, nicking our coal as we had forgotten to lock it up again. At least we only got blamed for not locking up. How could anyone do such a thing to a family who were relatively poor? I don't think Dad spoke to the next door neighbour again unless he had to. This neighbour had been very kind to us when we first moved there giving us our tea.

When Dad came home from work, there I would be. "Not well again, Jo?" Dad said and he would give me a cuddle and we would talk until it was time to get everybody up and Dad would go to bed. I used to love this time. The doctors told me later that my bronchitis was psychosomatic, as it was, according to them, attention seeking and when I felt insecure. It felt very real to me. I was given linctus by the doctor but I absolutely refused to take it, the taste of it was horrible so the rest of the family drank it. My nan bought Collins elixir, it was warm and lemony as it went down and I would not let anyone else have any of that. Also from Nan came the egg custard with nutmeg on top, no pastry when you were ill. (I have never been able to make one as well as hers ever). I was spoiled no doubt about it. My sister, Jeannette, hates egg custard and does not like it with or without pastry.

On a Saturday night, my nan, her sister, Hilda, and her brother, Albert, used to go down the *Black Boy's* pub in Colegate, which was right near the dole place at that time. It is now called *The Merchant* although it is not a pub anymore. They also used to go to the *Windmill* on Aylsham Road, owned by a woman called Lily, she was a fantastic lady, but old even then.

Great Uncle Albert had the most incredible blue eyes that I had ever seen; they were like a really blue sky with stars in them. Don't know where Albert lived at that time, but later he lived at the top of Penn Groove in the new-built flats, built just after the new houses.

Great Aunt Hilda lived on Waterworks Road, in a little cottage-looking place that still had gas lamps and no electricity. When she worked, it was at the Swan Laundry, which was on Waterworks Road. She never married as her fiancé had been in the war and all she had was a photograph and memories of him in his uniform. Aunt Hilda eventually moved into a flat not too far away on Causeway Close, with the bonus of electricity.

Apparently, one of Dad's aunties used to work as a prostitute and her pitch was up St. Stephens, whether this is true or not, I do not know but why would anyone in the family say it if it was not? I believe this lady was married, so if her husband knew, I don't know. I personally have nothing against prostitutes. I think that they do a good job and it helps to prevent more rapes. I think that it should be more like Amsterdam and legalised so they would pay taxes and have regular check-ups as a formality. After all, it is the oldest profession in the world

The dress I was wearing was a second-hand one from Sandra Young and it was lime and white checked. I absolutely hated lime green then and I still do.

Time to take what was called the eleven plus, an exam that would tell you what your next school would be. I hated it. I was not good at exams, I believe it had the whole curriculum in the one exam. It was quite a long time ago so you will have to forgive me if I am wrong. Anyhow, exam taken, and apparently I missed going to a high school by one point.

Me at eleven. I think I got Alan, the boy next door, to take this of me as he was playing about with a camera at the top of his garden and I said would he take one of me as I had not got many pictures of me when I was young. Not very good was he?

The next school I went to was Angel Road Secondary Modern for Girls. Yvonne S passed her exam to go to the high school, which I believe was the Blythe School then but because her friend was going to Angel Road she decided to go there, and then, you are quite right, her friend took the place that she had left free. We were taken there, to see where we would be, by a couple of teachers from Catton Grove and we were all herded into what they called their small hall.

All us girls were introduced to the teachers by the headmistress, Mrs. Diane Bagg, she was quite an attractive lady with grey-blonde hair. Let me see if I can get most of the other names right. Mrs Manhire was Deputy Head, a Mancunian (Manchester). Mrs Hay, maths teacher, very aggressive with the blackboard rubber, I had that thrown at me once or twice, a plump figure and she had been engaged for nigh on fifteen years then. I really hated maths. Mrs White, English teacher very slim. I loved English, although I was not too good at it. Mrs Martin, the French teacher, wore a white glove when she chalked on the board. I can still only do school board French to get by. The French talk far too quickly and I can only spot the odd word and know what it means. She used to make you stand by the door outside the classroom if you did something wrong, like talking when she was talking. You used to hope that the deputy/headmistress did not come past and see you or you would definitely get a detention. Mrs Fryer, the geography teacher, married when I was there and turned into Mrs Featherstone. I liked geography and I liked to think I was quite reasonable at it. Mrs Hagg, (yes really), was the art teacher, always going on about the eighteen inch waist she used to have although I don't think it was much bigger than a twenty-two then. I was not very good at art. I used to get my sister, Rosemary, to do it for me, and then I would sort of rough it up so it looked as if I had done it. Chimney pots and a scene from *Alice in Wonderland* are two that I remember. (My son is an excellent artist, gets it from his dad).

I am remembering a time when the class was in an art lesson and we sat four to a table. A girl called Sandra B, who was the niece of Ruby, was quite nasty to me. We did not get on at all and she kicked me under the table for some reason. She was an awful bully. She said to me, "Who you going to tell, your dead mother?"

Well I just burst into tears, Mrs. Hagg saw me and I told her what Sandra had said and she got sent to the headmistress. I did not sit near her again. Mrs Hagg also taught us to tie-dye and we made things from the material.

I made a handkerchief case for my dad, we stitched them up by hand with colourful wool in big hem stitch and put a name on it in cross-stitch. Nan used to put his nice laundered handkerchiefs in it; I believe my dad still had it when he married Ruby.

Mrs Wilson and Mrs Davidson were both domestic science teachers, (you know cooking and cleanliness in the home and kitchen). They taught us to iron – that's a laugh, they should have known that I had been ironing since I was nine. My nan taught me to iron a shirt properly, saddle of the back first, then collar and cuffs, then the rest of the back and then the fronts and if you are folding them up instead of putting them on a coat hanger, that too is a special way. Nan taught me when she was living on Hunter Road. She used to iron on one end of the kitchen table and plugged the iron into the light socket, as the wire had a bayonet head fitting so she could iron and there was like a double-ended socket on the light fitting so she could also have a bulb in it and she could iron anytime of the day.

I made a small loaf of bread which I thought was lovely. I don't know if Mrs Davidson was sorry for me as I had not got my cooking money with me that day; she said it was not very good so I did not have to pay for it but I could take it home anyhow.

I was very upset that she had said it was no good and my dad said, "You cut that up and I will take it for my tea break." I asked him next morning if it was OK and he said, "My lunch box is empty, it tasted all right."

I am quite a good cook these days but I have never attempted to make bread again, and to this day I cannot make a sponge however I try to make it, from scratch from a packet or by using gas or electric. In fact, I have had to put three sponges together to get one decent size when I made birthday cakes for my children.

Mrs Sergeant was the needlework teacher. She was young and pretty. I think that several of the teachers were jealous of her looks. I was not good at needlework and everything I made, especially on a sewing machine, I had to unpick. The first thing we did was sew our names on our gym blouses, so there was never any mistake whose they were. The next thing was making a white dress, again I had to get Nan to get Dad to get me money for the material. Nan duly went and bought a dress pattern with the material and a zip. All new girls had to make a white dress to wear for the end of their first year at the school, on opening day, to show off what we could do. Terrible nightmare of a job, I must have made that dress three times over by the amount of times I had to pull the machine stitches out and redo them. I cannot machine in a straight line, unlike my sisters who are very good at it. I am good at making things but still not on the dreaded sewing machine. I have made patchwork duvets for my children only using a sewing machine to put the back on it. I have turned curtains into duvets. I make table runners and table napkins. I revamp my clothes by hand.

Mrs Balls was the English drama teacher, very petite and old. Susan Jackson (same name as one of the pupils in class), started at the same time as I did, as a student teacher in the classroom of Mrs

Susan Balls and eventually took over when Mrs Balls retired. This was my first year classroom. At Christmas, in that first year at school, we put the play *A Christmas Carol* on and yes, you are right, as I was so small I got to play the part of Tiny Tim. The only thing was, that I kept swinging my legs under the table with nerves, why didn't they put a splint on my leg so I would stop.

But no, they put a tablecloth on so you wouldn't see my legs, very authentic, I don't think.

Mrs. Tingley was a sewing teacher and the typing teacher, the girls did not seem to like her much and it was said that they locked her in a cupboard and she had a breakdown but it is only hearsay. I never went in any of her classes so I would not know what she was really like. Mrs. Maxted was the religious instruction/education teacher, a very stern, strict lady. Once I was talking to the girl next to me, (Yvonne Smith). I know I shouldn't have been, but do you know what she did? She slammed the palm of her hand into my back. My back nearly went to my front and it hurt me badly but I would not let her see me cry. Think what would have happened today. She would probably have been brought up in front of the school board.

If I had told my dad what she had done, he would have given me a clip round the ear and said, "You probably deserved it."

Mrs. Thompson the science teacher, was a tall, thin and serious lady. I quite liked science, I wasn't much good at it but I liked measuring the rainfall every day. I did not like dissecting stuff though. I'm a girly girl. The science room was upstairs opposite the music room and when the lessons upstairs had finished and I was in a hurry to get to next one, I used to run down the stairs although you weren't meant to run anywhere. The girls always used to laugh at me and say, "Mind you don't take off, flappers."

It was the only time I was called that, it was because I used to wear my hair in a ponytail and my big ears would be showing.

Mrs Shepherd, the history teacher, was tall with glasses and a pock-marked face but she was quite nice. I liked history, thought I was good at it and I really enjoyed her lessons, they were really interesting.

There was also a gym teacher but I cannot remember her name. I do believe that she taught us how to dance reels and things as well when it was raining, as we could not do netball and sports. I cannot believe that I cannot remember her name, as she was quite memorable. I was the tiniest girl in the class and she used to scuff me up and throw me over the high jump bar to demonstrate to the other girls how to do the western roll (or was it the Fosbery flop?) and land properly. Wouldn't be allowed to do that sort of thing now. I could never climb the ropes, I think that I was a bit scared of the height and I never seemed to have the strength in my wrists to support me. You would think that, as I was such a lightweight, I would shimmy up no problem but I was not a tomboy. I was, and still am, very girly.

Mr. Crandall was the music teacher but I think he came a bit later, in my third year at the school. When he came into the school, we had a fire practice. It was quite a memorable one as Mr Crandall came out of the building, carrying the school secretary who had a wedding dress on and a sanitary towel looped over her ears, holding on the veil, it was hilarious. I did like the school secretary she was game for a laugh, although I cannot remember her name, she was always nice to me.

Mr Crandall was all sweetness and light when talking to the teachers, as he was the first man ever to teach at that school. I'm sure that we had a man who used to come in to tutor us in singing at St Andrews Hall with a lot of other schools but I can't think of his name. I think Mrs Manhire took us before that. He took the class when we all went on strike, he was a horrid man, either scratching his bum or picking his nose.

I believe that it started because of Pamela W, she would not sing on her own, or something like that, she had to go and stand near him. When she did not do it he pushed her back, none to gently, onto the desks and she fell back onto them and hurt herself, so we all went on strike and stopped singing in support of her. He went and got Mrs Manhire, who had become the head teacher at this time and when she came up to us we all sang as normal. We continued doing this for a time, at least three more lessons and in the end all the class got a detention but we never sang to our full potential for him ever again. I don't think what he did to Pamela ever got reported and if it did, I don't suppose that anything would have happened to him.

September came and with it the start of the school term. Dad had got a uniform from somewhere. I looked quite smart but I was petrified of going there on my own. Well Dad came up trumps and took me and there he met the headmistress who absolutely adored him. She took me under her wing, that's what some people called it, but the children prefer to call it Teacher's Pet. There weren't many in uniform and I felt a bit odd but I had to keep wearing it as Dad had gone to so much trouble. At this time, Rosemary was at Gurney School and John was at the Hewitt School, very good schools for them both. David, Stephen and Robert at the Norman. James and Jeanette were at Catton Groove.

On that first Monday, we were again in the small hall and we were sorted into classrooms. There were three different levels, GCS class was the one I was in, an RSE class in which you would learn to type amongst other things, and just the Form 1, which was for people who wanted to leave when they were fifteen. The lessons were not so hard in that class or so I was told.

We were then all put into a House with colours which you would be in all the way through the school. I was in St Bridget of Assumption, green in colour (Mrs Hagg's Team), they were all named after nuns, St. Cecelia, St Etheldreda, St Hilda and St. Ursula. Yvonne was in St. Etheldreda. The Head Girl was in St. Bridget. There were six but I can't remember the last one. At the end of the week in the main hall, it was called out how many points each team had and how many detentions we were given and you used to have to stand up in front of the whole school.

I was on Mrs. Hagg's dinner table as well. A girl used to stand at the entrance of the dinner hall to check your tickets and you would be on a table of eight. The dinner monitor used to have to go up and get the trays with the meat or fish dish, always fish on a Friday and a helper would get the tray with the veggies on it. They used to have their own kitchens and cooks there and it was from here that Catton Grove School got their meals. The head cook was Margaret D, who used to live on my road. She used to go Angel Road School and was such a good cook that she got the job after she left. The meals for Catton Grove School came from her kitchens. It was the sort of school where you had to have the knife in your right hand to eat, they would change them around if you had it in your left, not that I was left handed but I did feel sorry for those that were. I loved school dinners especially the stew with mashed potatoes, I hated liver and would not eat it however long it took. I used to try to get it on to someone else's plate, which was difficult, as Mrs. Hagg was there. I do eat it now but I really have to fancy it. I would not eat tapioca it was horrible. I still do not eat frog's spawn, as we used to call it.

I didn't like all the dinner time that you got, as I never really knew what to do, especially if a friend had fallen out with you and gone on to another friend. It is an awful thing to be in a three way friendship but it was always Yvonne in the middle. I never knew why she had fallen out with me as I was one that would not say boo to a goose, as often is the way. Yvonne was the youngest child of older parents and was very spoilt, always got her own way, always had money to spend in the tuck shop and always had nice clothes. She was very tomboyish and she carried it off well. I suppose I was a bit envious of her as she could do practically anything she wanted. Her father was in his sixties, so I should imagine that her mum fell for her on the change. She had an older sister, Grace, and two brothers, Fred and Richard. I had a crush on Richard; he was so handsome and a bit cheeky, blond haired and blue-eyed. He married a really pretty lady. I cannot remember her name but I know she set up a shop called Carmen's in Magdalen Street as Richard and his brother, Fred had a clothes stall on the Norwich Market at that time. When Fred got married, he and his wife, Pat, got a stall to sell old fashioned sweets.

Yvonne used to laugh at me, because at the time everyone used to celebrate my birthday on the fifth of July until one day I needed to see my birth certificate and found my birthday was actually the third of July.

I saw Yvonne when I was out shopping once, I had turned forty and I was shocked at the state of her skin, it was very lined just exactly how her mum's used to be. I was with my daughter at the time and I said to her, "Please tell me I don't look that old." Yvonne even laughed at me then. She said she had told her two boys, (she even got what she had always wanted in that department as well, but whether they were blond and blue-eyed, I don't know, she had ginger hair so I don't think it likely), that she had gone to school with a girl who did not know her own birthday.

Yvonne, before she was married, went on holiday with her fiancé and although they had booked two rooms they put them in together as they were both called S, so when she got married she did not have to change her name. I do not think it is fair that girls have to do that. I suppose that is how double-barrelled names came about.

I did not have many friends at school but those that I did have always had Yvonne in the middle and used to play us one against the other.

When I was about fourteen, we went to a guide's camp for about a week. Nan made me a sleeping bag from a feather eiderdown; it was very warm and cosy much better than the other girl's bags.

I did not like camping; they had great big, white bell tents, which six girls occupied. I was frightened by the night-time noises and I slept with the tent mallet beside me.

We went on walk trails, following animal trails laid for us and a cross-country run, following a stick and stone trail. Our tents were our teams and each tent had to cook for a day, for every one of the guides. I decided to cook a meal that my dad used to cook for us at home.

Sausage Potato and Onion soup.

One great big cauldron.

As many potatoes as you were allowed to use.

Sausages halved to make it look as you have got more.

Loads of onions.

These were all put into boiling water with salt and pepper to add flavour.

Put on the fire to cook.

Serve with bread and margarine, also as much as you were allowed.

Absolutely bloody marvellous nosh and filling.

Yvonne made instant whip for dessert.

I have only been camping once since then and I ended up sleeping in the car.

*

Many things happened at home in the four years that I was at this school.

The boys used to put one of the bed mattresses on the stairs below the window on the tenth stair down, before it turned the corner, they then proceeded to jump down on to it. James hurt his ankle doing this, badly sprained it. They just told Dad that he had fallen down the stairs. Dad must have believed the boys, as he did not use the persuader on them. The persuader was a black leather strap that Dad would use when the boys were trouble. Anyhow, dad piggybacked James to school so he wouldn't have the school board after him for keeping James off school.

The boys would dig holes in the garden, supposedly to bury rubbish, but they use to make tunnels, they made me go under one once, I hated it, I cried but they wouldn't let me out of the hole till I had done it, very claustrophobic. Anyhow, one day they had one of these tunnels, cousin Stephen was round playing with the boys, he was my dad's brother's boy. They tied a rope round his waist and yes, you've sussed it, the tunnel collapsed on top of him as they had not made the bridge thick enough, if they hadn't got the rope around him to haul him out, I'm sure we would have had a death on our hands.

This cousin, Stephen, had a brush with the law and told the police that he lived at our address. The police came round to our house and said, "I've just had your boy, Stephen, down the police station."

"No you haven't, my boy has been home here with me."

Stephen popped his head out.

"He's not the one."

"I know and it's not the first time it's happened, mistaken identity." Then the policeman left.

The boys always used to be making go-carts out of old prams and bikes. They used to have races on the path, never mind who was in the way as Jeannette and her Chinese skipping partners were one day. (Chinese skipping was done with a long bit of elastic and the girls jumping and stretching elastic about). Anyhow, the boys went charging in to them. The elastic tangled round the wheels and the girls were pulled along by the elastic around their ankles. All are scarred now.

Stephen had also been watching Zulus and made a spear from a stick and a knife and threw it at Jeannette, it ended up in her leg, another scar for her.

David also hit Stephen on the head with a promp/prop (the wood that held the linen up on the line) and it split his head open, with blood going everywhere. He put his head under the tap, washing the muck out of his head and they held Jeannette's new flannel over it, Jeannette was crying because they were using it, we did not often have new things, she screamed that they had better bring her flannel back from the hospital. It was as I said, we did not have much, so a new flannel would have meant a lot to us. There was never a dull moment at our house

The boys used to go over Western Road dump, beside the school and I went with them one light night. They had Stephen H with them and Stephen tried to kiss me when he got me on his own but I ran off. I believe he said, "I'll show you mine if you show me yours." No chance of that.

At that time, my dad's younger brother, Albert, who was married to Joan, (he was cousin Stephen's father, the one that nearly died in the tunnel), stayed unknowing to me. I found out when I was taking a cup of tea up to my dad. In the bed next to him, I saw this body with long blond hair, I put the cup of tea down and practically ran out of the room. I heard laughter behind me as I ran down the stairs and told Christine that there was a woman in bed with Dad. She came up with me and it was Albert in a long blond wig. I felt really stupid then. It was the first time I had heard my dad laugh in a long time so I suppose the deed did some good.

That was the laugh line all week at our house, and probably the whole street.

*

My brother, Robert, used to wet the bed after my mum died. I don't know if he did it before, as Mum would have been there to sort it out. I don't really think that it was the fact that he wet himself that made Dad mad, it was because Robert used to take the sheets and hide them under the bath, the side panel came off and they smelled when they dried out and we did not seem to have too many sheets to replace them. Well, one day I was in the house, when Dad was getting really angry with Robert and he went to hit him. Although I was not very big, I stood in-between them and got a punch in the mouth for my trouble. Robert probably doesn't remember it, or won't, but Christine told me that she also came across Dad trying to put Robert's head in the bath water where he was washing the sheets out and of course she stopped him. I forgive Dad (but whether Robert did or not I don't like to ask him as it could bring back bad memories of times best forgot), he was under a lot of pressure at that time as I can see now that I am older. He kept saying that he would take Robert to the doctor's about it but he never did. Why?

*

The boys used to lock me in the coat cupboard next to the airing cupboard. How I cried, I used to be in there for what seemed like ages. I'm sure they used to go out. I'm quite claustrophobic now, don't like going in lifts, I would rather walk up the stairs. I don't like my bedroom door shut when I sleep at night,

When I go on a plane I always get a headache and feel sick as I have fear of being enclosed, but I hide it as well as I can, I take loads of headache pills to dull the senses.

I still prefer that my bathroom door is open and I only shut it when I have company or go for a number two, as I don't like people hearing my toilet. I usually make sure music or the telly is on especially when I'm on holiday or staying at someone else's.

When I was fourteen, I had to go to the doctors as I was bleeding from my bottom and it was very painful to have a number two. When I got into the doctor's room, he examined me and put his gloved finger up my bum. The pain was excruciating.

"I should think it is hurting, you have split the wall of your anus."

He then went on to question me as to whether anyone had interfered with me down there. God, I thought, here we go again, everyone is obsessed with that sort of thing. I could only tell him that I think it was caused by holding in my poo so it did not plop and make a noise as it hit the pan. We couldn't put paper down there for it to land on, as we used cut up newspaper and it would block the toilet. Someone came to the back door and he told me not to be so silly and to drink plenty of water, He gave me some cream that I had to put up there.

*

We were supposed to take turns washing and wiping up and we did try to have some sort of a rota. I can remember waking up one morning with a saucepan thrown at me as it was still in the sink soaking and it wasn't even my turn. My dad could not stand dirty dishes in the kitchen.

In the winter, when Dad was on nights, he used to get me up and when I was up and dressed he would snuggle down in the single bed with the feather mattress that I slept on, so he did not need a hot water bottle

That would be about seven in the morning after he had made the fire up, made a pot of tea for us and called us ready for school.

I hated early mornings and still do.

In the summer, weekends and holidays, Dad slept in his own double bed and room. He always had a room at the top of the stairs so he could hear if anyone came to the door and so he could hear his mate Alfie tooting at mid-day.

Often when we came home from school, he would be in his chair, I say in his chair in a loose sense of the word, he would, in the winter, be sort of on his knees asleep with his head in the chair and his bum up in the air near the fire, good job we had a fire guard.

Dad would have made tea for the ones who were out to work and as we had a school dinner we just had sandwiches or boiled rice when he had brought home a load from work where crates had split open from loading or unloading freight at work. Dad also got hold of tea but it was Earl Grey, a bit perfumed, not to our tastes at all and you had to drink it quick to get rid of it. I do drink Lady Grey lemon tea occasionally now but plain rice you can keep it. One time it was a huge, great big lump of chocolate we had to break with a hammer it was so thick.

*

One evening when John said I had to go to bed and I did not want to go, he opened the stair door and threw me up the stairs. I caught my little fanny (not my bum as the Americans call it) on the stair rail and I screamed with pain and as I was screaming, the knocker on the front door went, John answered the door and there stood my nan.

"What the devil is going on?" she said, "I heard you screaming up the road." I told her what John had done and she proceeded to hit him with the umbrella she had with her. Saved by my nan again. I don't recall if she told Dad or if I did.

He would have felt the persuader for that.

Nan used to pop around occasionally, to keep an eye on us while Dad was at work and she would give him an update when he went round for his dinner twice a week.

My dad apparently paid my Aunt Joan (the one married to Alan) to come and clear up for us during the day but I can hardly remember her doing anything. One day she asked me to go and change the bed linen and I wouldn't so she slapped my face. (I did not like housework anyhow and I still don't. I am allergic to house dust, if I brush too hard at anything, I start to sneeze and my eyes blow up and I look as if someone has punched me in the eyes). I told her she was a lazy old cow as she was supposed to be doing it and of course she told my dad and I believe that I got a smack on the hand with the persuader.

I must have told Dad that she made us do all the work, as after that incident she did not come round as much.

Her husband, Alan, used to do most of the housework at her own home, so goodness knows how she got on looking after Lorraine.

*

Once when I came home from school there was this mongrel up the front window of the house and I was scared to go in as it looked really vicious

But it was actually a soft old thing, another stray that Dad had taken in (he was as bad as Mum in that way) because nobody wanted it and it was going to be put down. Gyp, the dog was called and it attached itself to Stephen, it was more his dog than anyone else's. It was a funny old thing, we used to bath it in the old tin tub that we had brought from the old house. When we had done this, we always tried to keep him in the house as he did not sleep outside, but as soon as one of the doors got open he was out like a shot and what did he do but race up the top of Jewson Road to the dump, that's what we called it (it's got a social club on it now). Behind that was the pig abattoir. (This is all built on now with houses and a Lidl store). He would roll in the pig shit and God, if it was not bad enough having the smell of the abattoir in the summer, he used to bring it home with him and then we would sling a bowl of disinfectant water over him.

He also pinned a little girl up against the fence once, in the cut and we had to send Stephen over to sort him out and I have just realised how traumatised that little girl probably was, I do hope she got on all right she must have been about six.

Talking of dogs, the dog that belonged to the Hedges, who, had a fruit and vegetable stall on the Norwich market, got stuck in Ruby B's (who married my dad a lot later down the line) dog Penny, a bitch and the men folk had to get them apart as a bowl of water wouldn't have worked. The Hedges were related to my Aunt Joan, Peoples' families always seem to live quite close to each other in the fifties and sixties it's strange how further apart families live now but I suppose it is progress, with more transport available to those who wish to travel.

Gyp use to walk to the shop with us and carry his heavy tin of meat home in his mouth, Chappie it was, and I couldn't bear the smell of it and it was a red colour as was his poo.

I'm quite frightened of dogs, as when I was just walking quickly down the road I had one bite my finger and I have a little scar on it. I still do not know why it bit me. Perhaps it was because I was swinging my arms and it thought I was going to hurt it. To this day, I have to wash my hands after I have made a fuss over a dog and will never understand how people can kiss one and let a dog lick them.

Christine at twelve, down Yarmouth with Aunt Joan

As you can imagine Christine being the oldest was very put upon, she got very stressed out as she was working at Harmers clothes factory at the time, and then coming home to do housework that Aunt Joan was supposed to be doing .I don't suppose Chris got paid for any of what she did.

As she was cooking tea one night, she and John were arguing, they used to do that a lot at that time, a clash of personalities, and she threw the pan of hot water and potatoes over John. He had a V-necked t-shirt on and to this day, he has never had a hair grow in that v at the front.

Christine used to fancy the boy who lived at the top of our road. I believe his name was David, she used to ask me to be at the gate and call her when he came down the road, she would pretend to come out and tell me that it was time to come in as it was a school night. Then I would leave her to go in and let her talk to him. I would earn a little bit of pocket money that way.

Christine at eighteen (beautiful)

I don't know how she kept so slim as she had a secret treat, it was a tin of Fussell's condensed milk, it was thick and sweet and she used to eat it with a clean finger as she said it tasted better that way, I have tried it but find it too sickly.

Christine had a boyfriend, around the corner on Palmer Road, I think his name was Roy, she did his shirts for him and I took them to his when they were done. I can only assume she did this out of love, as she had enough to do at home. Anyway, one day when he was around our house, I think it was an evening, waiting for Christine, he asked me how old I was, I think I was fourteen at the time, and he said that he had better keep an eye on me as I would be a right little cracker when I matured.

He frightened me but I looked a lot like Christine so he must have thought she was a bit of alright. I believe this was the only boy who ever broke her heart even though she was not engaged to him.

He used to ride past ours on a bicycle and it was kind of creepy. I was very wary of him.

She had another boyfriend who she was engaged to, called Barry. He was a good looking boy and was in the building trade. My Uncle Joe was a carpenter and so knew Barry. Christine was fifteen when she was walking down the road with Mary C, a girl who also used to live on Soleme Road, and he and another friend asked if they wanted a lift.

She went out with him for four years and would go out many times with Uncle Joe and Aunt Doreen. She would ask me to stay awake to let her in at night as she did not have a key.

Writing this, I have just remembered what they used to say to her as they went out in the car, it was don't leave any mushrooms on the back seat. I will not explain it, as I assume that most people will know what it means. I didn't until I went to work.

Christine had a falling out with Dad. Sometimes, when she came home from work, there would be no food to eat, so she decided not to give him his board money that week. Sunday came and he had still not said anything, she was getting ready to go out with Barry and then Dad tapped his hand on the mantelpiece and said, "Before you go out, you can put your board money on here."

Christine said, "No! There's never anything to eat!"

Dad then put on his leather gloves with the string-looking back and answered the door to Barry and Dad said, "Come in you are just in time to see me give her a good hiding."

"I don't think so, Mr Rowell," Barry said.

Christine did not do a thing; she just stood there waiting for it all to be over. I believe that she was on the verge of a nervous breakdown, she just wanted out.

Dad then punched Barry on the cheek, under his eye, and left scratch marks on his face from the string backs of his gloves. Then Barry grabbed hold of Dad's hands and got him on the settee so Dad could not move apart from his legs going nineteen to the dozen. Barry said, "I'm not going to let you go till you stop punching." So Dad stopped and Christine left home for eighteen months, living at Barry's mum's and I think that is what made them disengage, as he became more like a brother.

It was when she worked at Elmo's in Magdalen Street, Dad used to see if he could catch a glimpse of her and she used to hide up until he was gone. The Elmo's supermarket was another job, (they used to give out Green Shield stamps and you could buy things from the Green Shield Catalogue. Christine saved them and got a lovely dinner service for her bottom drawer), this shop was on Magdalen Street (now where the Oxfam shop is). I believe Christine was accused of having an affair with one of the married men who worked there, I babysat for him and his wife. Whoever accused Christine must have been looking through rose-coloured glasses, as he was one of the ugliest men I had seen at that time.

*

They finally did speak and Dad begged her to come home, she gave in and said, only if she could do the shopping. Dad agreed, so she paid for the shopping and took that as her board. You could get a lot for thirty shillings in those days.

Christine's first job was in Harmer's Clothes Factory on the sewing machines. She also had a part-time job as a silver service waitress for a restaurant called Princes near Tombland, they used to get searched in case anyone had stolen the cutlery.

While Christine went to work, the house seemed to get a makeover. We suddenly got a carpet on the floor, which was duly burnt by cigarettes within a week of getting it, I don't know who did that. I think the carpet was blue and we had some nice blue patterned brocade curtains, very posh they looked as we already had wooden pelmets, which came with the house. (This is where the old persuader was hidden later on, so Dad could not find it).

Christine had done this so she would not be ashamed when visitors/boyfriends came round. It must have taken quite a bit of money. Whether Dad gave her any money to go with it, I don't know. I believe that we got new wallpaper as well, a job my dad detested and when we ran out of paste, he used flour and water.

Then she went off to the Isle of White, to work in one of the hotels there, with her friend Linda, then she returned from there and she met her husband, called Millis, a Londoner brought up in Heigham I do not know if that is the right spelling. A handsome man with charm, he was a coachbuilder carpenter, was very good with his hands but what a funny first name – I have never heard of it then or since. Christine had had a quick wedding because of the usual circumstances. Christine had come home weeks earlier to tell Dad and I believe that she told Ruby B. first so she could let Dad know gently.

They had their wedding at St Luke's on Aylsham Road, in Norwich. She came down and stayed at ours while the banns were read out, although she lived in London, in Richmond. She had her mate Linda as a bridesmaid, who had bought her own dress, as Christine could not afford to buy it. Christine had hired her wedding dress. I think that she ended up with a cigarette burn in the train. I could not go out on the hen night as I was not old enough, that was a real downer as I was at work at the time and the age limit for actually going into the pubs had not yet been lowered. I can remember that it snowed and it was very cold.

When the service was finished and we all went outside, the men all rushed over the road to the little woods which had billboards on it, to have a pee, even the groom as they had been drinking before the wedding and all you could see was the men's head over the top of the boards.

*

John was asked to leave the Hewitt school (it was probably because he played truant too often but I really don't know) before he was quite the age to leave. He worked with my Uncle Albert, my dad's brother, as a painter and decorator and I do not think Albert was that nice to him. He always had to wait for his wages and I believe they were nearly always slung at him. He did not put up with that for long.

John is not one to talk about his past, but I know that he doesn't like to be ordered about and never has.

John used to go out at night and take the clock we had on the mantelpiece with him. He apparently went to see an older woman who lived in Shorncliff Avenue, just off Aylsham Road, and he came back in the mornings before Dad got home. This lady's name was Carol and she was a bit older than John, so I do not know how she met him but I do know that she had a son and they were both badly treated by the boy's father. John married Carol when he got a bit older and adopted the boy and treated him as his own.

Arguments with John were happening all the time in our house with Christine and me, why us two girls I will never know. I suppose personality clashes had a lot to do with it.

I remember the Saturday dinnertime that I was cutting bread from an unsliced loaf to go with the chips and beans we always had on a Saturday. John was swearing as usual, I cannot abide swearing, it is such a lack of vocabulary. I went in the lounge where the dining table was and told him to stop swearing or I would cut no more bread, I went back into the kitchen and he came up behind me to punch me and said, "I'm not swearing."

"Yes you did, you are always swearing."

I still had the bread knife in my hand when I raised my arm to protect myself and his hand went down on the knife blade, he was stunned into silence. I had to clear the blood up and he went back to the table, sat down, and then promptly fainted. The tendon in his hand had come out from his skin and we ran over the road to Ruby B's. I cannot remember what happened next apart from that he had it bandaged up .He is scarred on his hand, it's a purple colour and to this day he tells people I hit him with the knife, not that I was protecting myself from him.

David and John used to go strawberry picking in the summer holidays. A lorry used to pick people up at the shops on Woodcock Road .I wanted to go but Dad wouldn't let me, he said I was too small and I would get hurt, but I think that he wanted me home to do the housework. The boys would bribe me into washing or ironing a shirt for a bit of pocket money.

We would eat the strawberries they brought home, they were delicious, althoughI have a strawberry allergy that I didn't know about – we did not have the knowledge that we have now. At that time, I only use to get little spots and they looked the reverse of a strawberry; green with a red dot in the middle. I thought it was just teenage spots, this has got worse as I have got older and now I have breathing difficulties if I have anything with strawberries in it, and a rash if I bathe in anything strawberry based.

John and David used to both go to the T.A centre on Aylsham Road, up near where the Sunshine Bakery used to be. I don't think John enjoyed it much as he would have been ordered about.

John took this up as a job, working on the fields, as he was his own boss.

He ended up in Anglian Windows as a foreman at the Bowthorpe plant. It was one of the best paid jobs in Norwich for unskilled labourers. He got on very well with the owner as all the Rowell family did.

David later on joined the army; he looked so handsome in his uniform. He bought himself out before he did a third stint in Ireland. I think he became traumatised when on his second stint, he was out for the evening and instead of waiting for the bus to come, walked back to the barracks and in the morning he had to clear up bits of bodies as the bus stop had blown up and it could have been him.

I used to write to David regularly and he was a very nice person when he came home.

Once when David came home on leave, he borrowed Dad's mackintosh to go to a football game with Stephen and in those days a lot of the cars had sticky-out handles. David was waiting to cross the road and the car's handle got caught in his pocket and dragged David up the road and ripped the coat pocket. When the car eventually stopped and the driver got out, David stuck the nut on him and ran off. I hope the bloke he did it to will not read this.

He put Dad's coat back and Dad never knew how his pocket got ripped or did he and just made a joke of it?

He was very happy in the army especially when he was in Germany.

When David came home on leave, the local boys used to try to pick a fight with him, he actually spent the first hours of his 21st. birthday in a police cell. It was the 31st of December, the day before he was born on January 1st. The boys in the *Woodcock* pub were goading him as usual, so he left the pub and the boys came out after him. I'm not sure that the boys had time to do anything to him as someone else came out of the pub and the boys went off in a car, As they were driving off, they tried to run him over, calling abuse out of the window. David found an iron pipe on the ground and threw it into the back window of the car, a stupid thing to do but I suppose his dander was up. Unfortunately there was a police station just a little further down and he got caught by the bobby on the beat. He was let off with a caution as he had just got back from Ireland.

David and John in the back garden of Jewson road

David in his army uniform

When he came out, he used to have to go up to London, I believe as he was on standby if we had a war. I think he had to do this until his contracted years had gone, not many left at that time, maybe three.

David was paid for this journey, it was to make sure that his kitbag was up to standard.

Rosemary sitting on the porch at Aunt Joan's
with Jeannette and Lorraine

David worked for the council for a bit as an electrician; how he ever got that job, I will never know as he was colour blind.

David worked for Bullard's Brewery after that, it was situated down near the social security office, down near King Street. I suppose he was what you would call a drayman but it was on lorries not horses.

I believe that David met his wife, Carol, at a nightclub, in Magdalen Street. Carol worked at the social services offices. David also ended up in the Glass Room at Anglia Windows.

Rosemary Elsie, the tomboy, or so I thought but everyone thought she was quiet, I suppose we all see people different. She went to the Gurney School, quite a decent one, she was very intelligent, I do not know what grades she got but I expect that she had to leave school like the rest of us as. Dad would not have been able to keep us on as he needed us to work and fend for ourselves.

Rose used to fancy a boy round the corner on George Pope Road, I believe it was Tab H, if that was his real name, I don't know, but if it was him I thought that he was real handsome and looked like a film star. Rose used to go for a walk round the block, I used to tag along and she used to pretend that she had been looking for me and found me as she walked past the boy's house. Alfie H used to throw bricks at us, so I don't know what all that was about. I know now that Tab H used to follow Christine and Rosemary down the road and it was Christine that Tab liked but Christine had told Rose that it was her he was following, as Christine didn't like him.

Rosemary first had a job in the wages office at Harmers where Christine worked on the sewing machines.

Rosemary or 'Rose', as we used to call her, went to work up in the office of Harmer's in the wages department, maybe Christine got her the interview as she worked there. I thought it was fantastic one of ours in an office. Office work was a very prestige job in the 1960s, a nice, clean atmosphere. She also worked in a shop office, I believe it was called Moore's and when Dad got a Mutual cheque, it was one of the shops that you could spend it in.

There were not many but you could get clothes from these stores. It was one of those where the assistants put the money in a container with the bill of sale, written in duplicate, and it would whoosh up a long tube and end up in the office. It would come back with paid on the bill, with change, or what you had left on the cheque to spend.

Dad would have a man from the mutual come round to collect money every week to pay for the cheque and this was where we got most of our clothes from, if they were not to be second-hand.

Rose went off into the army and I think she learnt to drive and drove trucks about.

Once when Rose came home, she brought a fellow army bloke with her called Heinz, so he must have been German, very handsome and my dad and Heinz got on very well. Dad used to call him fifty-seven, my dad never held grudges like that. We thought that he would be Rose's boyfriend but she said not.

Rose came home in a borrowed Mini car, amazing how people borrowed each other's cars in those days without any fuss, and I think some of us piled into it and went to Hunstanton. It was a lovely day, playing on the beach, rounders and the long jump of all things, but it kept us happy.

Rosemary met her husband in the army, he was John Smith, the most common name in England. John was an army butcher from Wolverhampton. Unfortunately it was another quick wedding, only my dad and Nan went to her wedding as it was too far away for all of us children to go. Rose got married in a cream suit with fur on the collar.

They stayed living up in Wolverhampton.

Rosemary contracted German measles when she was pregnant and her baby was born with a beautiful upper body but its two legs went into one, it was a still birth so I suppose it was meant to be, stuff happens for a reason, so they say.

After Christine had had her baby, Robert went to live with her because, if he hadn't, he would have ended up in borstal, which was a detention place for naughty boys under sixteen. Robert and James used to go out at night to the bakery on Aylsham Road and nick cakes out of the van and bring them home. I must say they were lovely so I suppose all us children were accessories to the crime, as we knew about it. They used to hide the cakes under the old bath but they never stayed there for long, not with all of us. God help us if Dad had ever found out. They also used to go and nick stuff from the Corona factory, but they were caught and a policeman came round to speak to Dad. The constables on the beats got to know more people then, and we actually respected the police and their jobs.

Dad had to go to court and plead for the boys not to go to borstal but instead for the boys to live with their elder sisters who would have guardianship of them. Rosemary took James to live with her in Wolverhampton.

So, Robert ended up at Christine's; their birthdays are on the same day so Christine said that Robert was her birthday present one year.

I think that the impression everyone got from Christine was that she was quite well off money wise and so Dad did nothing to help out with the transfer of Robert into her home .The one thing that she did do for Robert, was to take him to the doctor's to see about his bed wetting

Apparently, Robert would go into too deep a sleep to wake himself up to go to the toilet. The doctor gave him some tablets to take and he was cured I don't know how long he took the tablets for but think, if my Dad had taken Robert to the doctor's then all that stress would have been gone and Robert would not have had the hidings.

Christine also had his feet seen to as his toes had begun to curl, his toes were broken and metal pins put in them to straighten them out so it was a good thing for him to have been at Christine's, although all the while he was there he just wanted to come home. Staying in a shed, instead of going to school.

Christine lived in a sort of flat, it had only one bedroom so Robert slept on a bed settee in the sort of kitchen/lounge and they shared the bathroom with the tenants upstairs and there was no real partition from the door/hall way to their abode.

When Robert was up there he learnt the butchering trade.

Dad gave Rosemary quite a lot of help; she had new clothes to take with him. James had a room in the attic of Rosemary's house and used to play truant a lot of the time. Being up in Wolverhampton, there were many different cultures in the classrooms and a white person was in the minority although John and Rosemary seemed to get on all right with it but their house always smelt of curry from the house next door, so I was told. James also just wanted to come home and he played truant many times until Rosemary caught up with him one and actually took him to school herself.

James of course learnt the butcher trade, isn't it weird that both those boys did?

*

I keep talking about Ruby B, well my dad started going out with her in secret, they had assignations well away from the street and met outside pubs in the city .She had five children; Carol, who was oldest, around about same age as my sister Christine, then there were Janet and John the twins, aged as Rose. Then came Paul the same age as John, and Diane a year older than me. We all used to play in the street together and I do mean on the road, playing rounders, British Bulldog and Chicken. We used to call Paul, Bagsy, as he was always saying I bagsy to be this or that.

We all got on reasonably well together so you could say that we were being nurtured into a big happy family.

Dad started calling in on Ruby for his early morning cup of tea and maybe a bite to eat, and he used to go round after he had been to the pub. We often used to come home from school and he would still be round there, we had found out that they were an item.

When I was around the age of fourteen, we started to swap Sunday newspapers. One week I would take them round Ruby's, making sure that I had combed hair and a looked reasonable in my appearance, (vanity of course) and the next Sunday John B used to come over to ours. Although he had a turn in his eye, I thought he was most handsome. Later on, when we were related as such, I asked him why he had never asked me out and he said, "I didn't think that you would have gone out with me and I did not want to get rebuffed."

I told him, I had fancied him like forever, but I could not have asked him as it was not the done thing.

When I was out to work, he married a girl called Pandora and I don't think she was quite the thing, as I saw John, one night, looking for her down the Melody Rooms, a place that he never would go to normally. Anyhow I think he found out she had been lying to him and they got divorced. What do you think happened next? My brother, Robert got involved with her. He was a bit younger than her, so it was a bit like cradle-snatching and he married her when he was old enough. So that was my step-brother's ex-wife marrying my brother. Talk about keeping it in the family!

I still think John is handsome, even in his sixties and I get on really well with his second wife. His wife does know that we fancied each other when we were younger and she knows that nothing came of it

We started going round Ruby's for Christmas tea and at Easter. It was nice having someone who had made mince pies and sausage rolls for you and turkey sandwiches and we played board games as well as watching the television.

We girls used to go to Ruby if we ever needed anything from my father, she would talk him into giving it to us or talk him down from being angry with us.

One incident that I remember, is when Jeannette shared a bedroom and a double bed, it was one of those at street front over the top of the little flat. It faced the flats on the opposite side of the street and every night when we went to bed, whatever time it was, and we went to shut the curtains, there was a boy who was, no other words for it but, playing with his penis for all to see. I did not think this was right so I slipped over the road to Ruby's to ask her to come and see this. So we slipped in the back door, as it was the way where he could not see us from where he was standing and she saw what we saw and she said that she would deal with it.

The next thing that we knew was that a wardrobe was put in front of his window, so it was Ruby to the rescue. I think the boy's father was a dustman; he was called Soapy, so maybe his name was Johnson, I can't remember his mother being about.

Jeannette had a gollywog, and the boys, especially Stephen, used to get it and put string around its neck and drop it from the upstairs window and get it to tap on the window to upset Jeannette and she could not reach it, as she was little. She loved that gollywog. Perhaps that is why they did it, as they had nothing that they loved like that.

Another incident involving Jeannette that happened on a weekend, I used to go for walks and I chased her down the road as I did not want her with me and she got stung by a bee, three times on the neck she insists that it was a bee but I always thought they could only sting once. She said it was too big to be a wasp, anyhow I got blamed for that as she went howling around to Ruby's to sort it out and I just ran off out of the way and I got a smack off my dad for chasing her anyway.

Right so I can control bees now, and what they do.

*

The school went on a trip to London, to see the waxwork museum and the history museum and yes, I got to go, it was the first and last trip I had with a school. Nan arranged everything for me, and I stayed at hers for the early morning start. Good old Nan, she tried to make me eat breakfast but I could not eat, I never can eat breakfast so early in mornings. I know it is supposed to be the best start to a day but it is not so nice second time around so, as usual, I took it with me to eat later on the coach. I sat next to Yvonne and, as usual, she had a wonderful packed lunch, made my nice one that Nan had prepared for me, meagre looking compared to anyone else in my class, so I suppose they thought I just ate less.

Anyway, I had my barley sugar that my Nan had got me to combat the travel sickness, which did work.

On the way home late at night, the latest I had ever been allowed out, I was sitting next to Yvonne who said she did not feel well and we had to get her the coach bin to be sick in. I thought that it was because she had eaten too much, as she had a very big lunch box with her but she said not and she was bright red. It turned out that she had German Measles and I decided that I would go round to see her and I did something that I had never done before, I did not go to school that day. Her mum went to work so I spent the time with her trying to get German Measles so I would not get them if I was ever pregnant (as I knew this is what had caused the birth defects in Rosemary's baby) but I did not get them I will never understand why.

Yvonne and I would sometimes go on the Waterloo Park on the way home from school, in by the Angel Road entrance. Don't ask me why as I did not like going high on the swings as it made me feel sick. One night, after four, that was what time we finished school then, we were sitting on the swings and this man came out of the men's toilets with his flies undone and his penis out. He asked us if we wanted to play with it, so we ran off and found a park keeper and told him what had happened. He went back to the swing park but the man had gone. He did look over the rest of the park but could not find him. I never told my dad, or anyone else when I was young, about what had happened as I did not want to be stopped from going to the park, as that is what would have happened.

At the end of the third year we had exams and my results were OK but not brilliant. One that particularly miffed me was the music one as I was quite good at music and singing but I believe that Mr Crandall marked me down because I would not sing solo in a play they were putting on about Hiroshima. It was called The Green Children or something like that but I did not like to single myself out for attention like that. I said before about Mr Crandall's behaviour and his pettiness, he would hardly have chosen me to do solo if he did not think I was good would he?

My history and religious instruction weren't too bad either but I didn't think I would have made good G.C.S.E. exam material.

*

In my last year at school I opted out of taking G.C.S.E. exams as I knew Dad would not be able to afford it, I wanted to get out into the big wide world and I knew Yvonne was not staying on.

We saw a lot of films on childbirth and sperms swimming about to get pregnant and how not to get pregnant and the best precaution is not to do sex at all. We watched women giving birth and I felt sick to my core. I cannot watch women giving birth even now, it makes me cringe and feel sick even though it is supposed to be a beautiful event.

We used to have to shower after gym, in the communal showers and I hated it as everyone could see your bits and pieces and my nan had cajoled my dad into getting me a bra. I only wore vests up until then and when she did get them I had two, beginners bras, they were white and the cups were like a stretchy material so they grew as you grew, like one size fits all and I was very proud of them – the bras not my breasts. Anyhow, one day in the changing room, I had this tall, big girl called Raquel (I'm sure that was her name) laugh at me as I had the bra on she said, "What on earth have you got that on for? You have not got anything to put in it."

I replied to her in a way that I never take people on, "At least I will not have them swinging about like yours when I do get bigger breasts," I did say this in a loud voice so the other girls could hear, to embarrass her the best way I could and they shouted out that I was right. She thumped me on my arm and went to the other side of the changing room.

The next gym day she actually had a bra on, so I suppose I did her a favour, as I'm sure it did her good later in life.

*

During that fourth year, in a class where you would be leaving at the end of it, the work was easier and you just ambled along. Yvonne and I put a play on called The Burglar, it was a play that only had two parts, it was a comedy. The scene was two people in bed. Yvonne was the man as she had short hair and was bigger built than myself. George was his name and Mildred, that was me, and no our last name was not Roper as in the TV series, we had no last name .We were asleep with the lights out and I was supposed to have heard something downstairs and woken George up to go see, with a great deal of fuss. I of course kept up a running commentary while George went down the front stage stairs and disappeared from view. I was not word perfect, and I had the sketch in my magazine on the bed but it fell off with the blankets as the covers got thrown off. I had to ad lib, much to Yvonne's disgust, but she managed it quite well with a lot of noise and grumbling as you would do if you were sent off in the middle of the night to tackle whatever had made the blooming noise. Well, in the last rehearsal, when Yvonne was coming back up the stairs to bed, her pyjamas fell down around her ankles. The cord holding them up had broken and all our class exploded with laughter, Mrs Jackson asked if Yvonne would be able to do it again and she did not know if she could as it was a bit embarrassing, so none of the class knew if she would or not. Good old Yvonne, she did and it was so good to hear all of the laughter from parents as well as the school and we felt right proud that something not in the script actually worked. The burglar, well that was the bloody cat bringing a mouse in as a present.

*

Girls who stayed to school dinners were not allowed out of school during the dinner break unless they had a note from their parents but, as fourteen year olds, most were a bit rebellious.

One of the girls lived over the other side of the park on Waterloo Close. She had a really big, smart house and the inside furnishings were really nice, her mother went to work so I suppose she was a latch key kid.

We were walking along and I was a bit behind as I did not really want to go but I believe Yvonne said that I would be a chicken if I didn't, they all did this regularly and this was my first time.

Well a good job I was behind, as I saw one of the teachers coming a far way off and I shouted to the girls what was happening, then I went and hid behind a hedge and they just sauntered past the teacher. After the teacher had gone past, I ran after the girls and they just said, "So what."

I said, "Won't you be scared when you go back?"

They said, "No what can they do, expel us we are leaving anyhow." So we carried on to the girl's house.

I was really frightened, not only of what the teachers would say but what my dad would say if it became known that I was flouting school rules. That afternoon, Miss Hay, who was deputy head as well as our form teacher, said she wanted the names she was about to read out to stand up. The girls standing up were seen out of school grounds that day and that they all had detention and wouldn't be receiving a school leaver's certificate.

They all glared at me but no way was I going to stand up and say that I was also there when she obviously had not seen me. I'm not a brave person, just stupid now and again. (Girly girl).

A school certificate is what the girls received to say that they were capable of holding a job down, like a reference from the school.

Yvonne did not speak to me for a bit after that until she needed someone to boss about. I used to call her Smith's crisps and she would say, "I'll get you for that."

Until she had made up with me, one of the older girls, the sister of Shirley H, (I'm blowed if I can remember her name), walked home with me and would call for me to go to school. "She won't be with you forever," Yvonne used to taunt me.

They lived just up the road from me but Shirley did not go to the same school .I think she went to Blythe School. She must have been brainier than me.

The Christmas before I left school, Dad gave me a provident cheque, the one that you could spend in shops to get clothes at Moore's, where Rosemary once worked. I went with my nan of course, she was like a rock for me and I relied on her completely. I got a dark blue, wool dress that had four tight pleats in it and a pair of patent leather court shoes, smallish heel, it was very hard to find decent shoes as I was a size 2. Well I looked the bee's knees in the outfit. I was so pleased. I bought some plain underwear as well and new pyjamas, I never had nightdresses. They are too frivolous and not very practical in our cold house. New brush and comb, because mine had had it, oh and handkerchiefs of course. I already had a coat that I wore for school, which I actually liked, it was a dark blue and it had big buttons down the front, a nipped in waist and a huge collar, it was a bit old fashioned but I liked it. It had been a hand me down of course.

About a month before we left school, the fourth form leavers were sent to the employment exchange to see what job they were capable of. I don't know if we were sent in pairs or what. I was very scared and thought what if they say I'm useless and I can't get a job or they say I'm too tiny, like my dad always said.

Well, there was a lady sitting behind the desk and we had to take our birth certificates with us – that was when I must have found out that it was the third not the fifth of July. She spoke to me to find out about me and what I could do. She had one of those flip roll files that had vacancies on them and she said, "I have a factory job here," I did not want a factory job as I knew I would not be able to stand the smells and the men swearing as well as a few of the women.

The next job she looked at was a shop job and I said to her, "I'm not very good with maths."

She replied, "Just go to the interview and see how you get on."

I said, "OK." My heart was on the ground as I was very nervous. The phone call and the appointment was made, so off I went to the interview. (It's a pity they don't do that sort of thing now at the job centres, which would indeed help a lot of people get their foot in the door of a lot of places. Even if they were told they were not successful candidates, at least the job centre would be earning the right to say they were helping people, which I do not think they do, having had experience later in life of the dole.)

The shop was little Woolworth's, in Magdalen Street, opposite which is now the Oxfam shop (so called little as the main store was on Rampart street near St. Stephens in Norwich). I went in. I had never being so scared in my life. It had a long wooden floor and I had to go right through to the end near the stairs and there was a little office, which was the cash office and duly handed my card over to the lady in the box and she took me up the stairs to the manager's office.

Mr Linley his name was, and he took me in a room near the top of the stairs and gave me this test and it was fractions, like how many buttons, which were a farthing each (yes farthings were still about, four to a penny), and how much a foot of ribbon would cost at so much an inch.

I am not good at exams and my palms were sweating. They gave me a glass of squash and I had to wait in a little room attached to the kitchen that served as a canteen, they were going to tell me if I had the job there and then. I had calmed down a bit and he came in about fifteen minutes later, he came out to see me and said I was the best applicant he had seen for this position and I could have the job if I wanted it. Wanted it? I was over the moon. I must have done the test OK. Back to school I went, as I had to finish the day off and had to tell that I had got a job starting the first week of leaving school.

Most of the girls were going to have some time off before starting work, no such luxury for me.

There was a girl at the school called Glynis S, no relation to Yvonne, she heard me say that I had not got much to wear suitable for work and she said she had some clothes that she had grown out of. I think she felt sorry for me and said they were only going out to the next jumble sale if not, as she had grown out of them, so I might as well have them if I wanted. So I went home from school with her and there was a lime green skirt, the style was excellent it was short mini like and had a sailor button do-up at the front, it hung on my hips but it did not have a waist band, so it looked OK. As you know, I hate lime-green but it seems to be my forte in life to have to make do with what people gave me and I was grateful, although I don't appear to be. There was also a pair of brown, stretch trousers like trews, with stirrups on them, they were too long but I turned I them up. Yes, I can do hand sewing when I must. Along with these were a white blouse that would go with the skirt, just a short-sleeved button through, so that was another outfit to wear.

I don't think we had the charity shops about like they have now, only jumble sales. Still they went to a good home. Me.

I would be earning money even though it was only four pounds and ten shillings a week, a great deal of money for someone like me.

Thirty shillings would have to go for my board money, leaving me three pounds to myself, how lucky was I?

Well I must have been pretty stressed out when I had the interview, as a week later I went to the school toilets one dinnertime and there was blood in my knickers. I was mortified, what was I to do? I had to scrunch up the toilet paper to make it soft as it was that Izal, shiny sort, with not a very nice smell. I always scrunched it, as it seemed to make it a bit softer, (it was still one up on what we used at home), put it in my knickers and hope that it stayed in. The next thing I had to do was get to the secretary's office without anyone seeing me, as I knew that she would have something I could use. Some hope. Yvonne saw me and wanted to know why I was going there. Talking of sanitary wear, I can remember my sister actually making these towels from cotton wool and a sort of stringy muslin, must have been cheaper to make as at that time they only had Dr Whites that I could remember and Tampax.

Anyway, the secretary saved the day and gave me a sanitary towel and two pins so I could pin it in my knickers. When I left school that day, I went around to my nan's, who by that time, had moved to Berner's Street, off Junction Road, into a two bedroom flat, which was really cosy for her, although it was on the first floor. She came with me to the chemist and bought me a packet of Dr Whites and a cotton belt with hooks on it for the loops to go on to, must have been a man to invent that bit of torture. You could see when anyone had these pads on as they were so bulky, so embarrassing. Nan obviously got the money from my dad as the next thing I know, Ruby was telling me that Dad had said to her, 'My Josephine has become a woman'. "Why was he so proud of that?" I said to Ruby, "My God I hope he has not told anyone else."

Next day at school, Yvonne brought in a Tampax and I said "How do I put it in?"

She said, "I usually put my foot on the toilet seat so it opens the legs wider and you push the cardboard tube in then push with your finger inside the tube so it goes up straight." Oh yes she was speaking to me by then. Well I did this, my God it was so painful, and I could not get it in right, although I told her that it was OK and thank-you for bringing it in as I did not want to appear stupid in front of her. She did see me put it in the incinerator she thought it was the towel that I had put in.

Did I need this just before starting work?

Yvonne and I kept in touch after we left school and her parents sent her on a training course at Grovesnor House on Prince of Wales Road, to learn how to use a comptometer. All to do with numbers, like an adding up machine, she had a month off before she started this. Then she got a job at Lamberts Wholesalers on Ber Street, it dealt with cigarettes and other items like chocolate, sweets etc. Lambert's had various little shops around this time, like the delicatessen in Gentleman's Walk opposite Jarrold's and the smokers shop opposite the market.

*

Monday the 22nd July arrived and there I was four foot nine inches, size two and a half shoe, and measurements thirty one and a half, twenty inch waist and thirty two hips, and weighed six and half stone. I felt really tiny to be stepping out into the big wide world, not even an adult yet.

I put on my blue dress with the shoes and went off for my first day. I walked as I did not have money for a bus, we opened at nine o clock, closed at five, and we had Thursday afternoons off, as it was early closing day for most of the stores at that time. One Saturday in four off. You went in at the main entrance, as the manager would have opened up already, and up to the first floor into a sort of locker room where I was issued with an overall, green of course but not lime green. Mr Linley took me round to meet the other colleagues and I was put on the haberdashery counter, which consisted of buttons, ribbons, snacks, hooks and eyes etc.

The long, brown, wooden counter was about four feet six high so you could only see me from the neck up and my Dad always went in to the main city on a Monday and he thought he would pop in to see how I was getting on. The next thing I heard was laughter, as my dad went into like a half bend, he was laughing so much when he finally spoke to me he said, "Sorry for laughing, princess, but I did always say you were too little to work, but you'll grow." And off he went, I'm sure he spoke to the manager and told him why he was laughing, then off he went waving cheerio.

Lou, who was the lady who was on the counter with me, was very nice and kind and taught me the ropes so I could understand and not to be frightened to ask if I was unsure about anything, as we all had to learn. There were not many staff in that store, only three of us on that big back counter, the next third of the counter had jumpers, cardigans, underwear, stockings, ties, belts etc. The next third had all electrical stuff on it, different size wire, light shades, bulbs, batteries and gardening stuff.

Right at the end of this was the little cash office, the girl in there was lovely but I don't remember her name, there were stairs next to the office, which led up to a cloakroom and the canteen room where you had to pay for any rolls or coffee and tea that you had.

In the middle were the sweets, Pick and Mix and every other sweet thing you could think of. The Monday I started, I saw this couple, (I was told later that they were lesbians I did not really know what they were, but I did not like to say), come in and they took a handful of sweets from the Pick and Mix and ate them as they went round. No one could do anything about it as they did not leave the building with them, only in their tums and they left the wrappers on the floor for someone else to pick up. Along the right hand of the store were groceries, not a vast amount but enough as we were the type of store that had everything.

I was so very nervous using the till, as it was a big responsibility and it did not add up like our tills of today do. You could have pencil and paper, which was essential really, and you kept it beside the till to use if you couldn't do it in your head. I did use my head quite a bit of the time but the fractions were the worst. It is like they say, if you have to do it, practice makes perfect, well not perfect but better. Eleven o'clock was my elevenses and I got to know a few more people, like the storeroom ladies: there were two of these and a boy called Jason who was a bit older than me but he lied a lot and was caught out on many occasions. My dad would have called him a bit of a rum'en.

We had dinner at one o clock, a lot of places shut for dinner so you could either go for a walk or stay in and eat your lunch. I had sandwiches that I had brought from home, as I did not have any money to use for their canteen.

The shop shut at five and we then had to make sure that all the goods were tidy, you know, ribbons rolled and buttons in their proper boxes and then put white sheets over all the merchandise to stop them from getting dusty and then it was time to go home.

I walked home and good old Dad had done my favourite for tea, shepherd's pie with cabbage and processed peas, my dad was a really good cook and it was only those who went out to work that got the cooked dinner at night time, as the rest would have had theirs at school lunch time.

Dad did not like it, as I always made a sandwich (I don't do it now but I would dearly like to, much too fattening and I actually have enough on my plate now, so I don't have to fill up) out of some of it to soak the gravy up, lovely grub. We never had a pudding, as Dad could not have afforded them.

Well the week went on and I got better, not so nervous and stressed out talking to customers, and everybody was quite friendly.

My first week's wages, it was wonderful. That Friday, Yvonne came round in the dinnertime and said she was going to see her sister-in-law who had a shop called Carmen's, did I want to go with her to spend some of my money. Did I? Just stop me, my own money to spend minus Dad's board, which left me three pounds. We went in and she had some lovely things, I suppose that it was what we would call a boutique.

I found some wide legged turquoise trousers with a buttoned flap like a sailors trousers with no waistband, which I liked, a thin, black, sleeveless polo neck to go with it and my black shoes. I thought I looked wonderful, but I could not afford to pay for everything at once so as I was Yvonne's friend she said I could pay half now and the rest next week, as I would need money for the rest of the week to get by.

So I could take them home and show everyone my new clothes, which I had not had very often. Dad was pleased for me and then he said, "I hope you have still got your board money." Which I did, as I had put that aside before I went shopping, I wouldn't have dared not to have had it.

Later on, when I had more money, I bought a pair of brown trousers, wide bottoms, and on bonfire night we, Yvonne and I, went up to St. James' hill and started to climb up from the roadside. I was really nervous, I have never liked loud bangs since I was little. Mother used to get us to hide under the table when we had thunderstorms. We were half way up and a firework banger came hurtling down the hill, just missed my face, banged onto my leg and burnt my trousers. I was very upset, I went home and left Yvonne there with some friends.

Why did I not listen to my dad? He had told me to stay in the garden with the bonfire that the boys had made.

On the first Saturday afternoon on which I did not have to work, Yvonne and I went roller-skating at Plumstead Road skating rink, behind the Co-op. This was the first time that I could actually get a bus instead of walking there. Which was quite nice: although I could not skate well, I did enjoy it. They did do snacks there although I never had any. It was very boisterous with all the boys there and I always skated around the edge of the room so I could quickly hold onto something if need be, Yvonne was an excellent skater and had her own white boots, I just had the hired ones, which were the strap on ones.

I would skate on my own and when they did the line skate, I tried to be off the floor but I did not always manage it. It was a line of skaters with a really strong skater in the middle and they would collect people on the way round and add them to the line and woe betide you if you were the end person, where I usually ended up if I had not been quick enough to get off the floor.

God it was so fast and it frightened the hell off me and I used to hold on as tight as I could but the person who had caught me would let go and I would go crashing into the barriers. I could not stop very well as I did not have the rubber stops on my skates.

I used to go baby-sitting every other Saturday night when we had finished skating. Yvonne would catch her bus home and I made my way on foot to my Uncle Dennis', Dad's brother, and his wife Pat, they lived on Graham Square in a three bedroom maisonette on the big Heartsease Estate. My Uncle Dennis had married late in life, and had married a divorced woman with a child. She was a very brainy person was my Aunt Pat, she knew a bit about everything you needed and if she didn't, she would find out. Jacqueline was her daughter's name and I taught her to read but she was gifted that way and started early as I did. By the time she was four, she could do all the puzzles everyone had bought her in double quick time, but there was something a bit wrong as she was obsessed by death. Not normal for a four year old, a bit morbid, but apart from that she was a beautiful child, she had lovely blonde hair and her eyes were like brown velvet. Aunt Pat got pregnant and I did actually notice that her usual figure in her pencil skirt had got a bit tight and she had difficulty doing it up. Pat had another daughter they called her Denise the nearest they could get to Dennis.

*

As I was a junior member of staff, I was used as a runabout, which I enjoyed more than being behind the counter. One of these many tasks was to go up into the stockroom if a customer wanted a certain item, to see if we had the colour/size etc. The two old girls, I say old, (old to me) but I suppose they weren't really, they were in their fifties (as I am now in my fifties, I don't think it's old at all). I believe they were sisters, one was a little bit slower than the other but it was probably why she had a job with her sister, but I liked them both very much, they were so funny.

For instance, one day I went up to see them in stockroom and what I needed was on a top shelf, I think it was a lampshade and she went up some steps and to my amazement she did not have any knickers on, my God, what a sight.

I was laughing and she said, "What's the matter with you?"

I said, "You haven't got any drawers on." (Drawers is what my nan always called them).

"Bloody hell," she said, "I thought it was a bit breezy down there, must have forgotten to put them on after I'd been to the toilet first thing. I was in a bit of a hurry as the alarm didn't go off and I had to catch the bus."

"Well we sell plenty of drawers here, you'll have to buy a pair, you can't work up here with none on, what if Jason sees you haven't got any on?"

She said, "It will give him a treat won't it."

"Some treat, it will give him the fright of his life," I laughed.

She then proceeded to lift her skirt and give me a Moonie. (Showed me her bum, in all its glory). She apparently did buy herself some, her sister told me, and she put them on her chitty for the week. Do you think that she had Alzheimer's? It wasn't the sort of thing that you would know in those days. When talking to her sister, she said that she had been dropped on her head as a baby.

The chitty was a list of things you had had during the week, such as rolls for lunch and the odd thing bought in the store during the week. You paid for them at the end of the week when you went upstairs to get your wages and they would take out what you owed them before you got your money. I don't think that we even got a discount, maybe you did but it would have only been about five percent.

Work life went on, and after I had been there about a month, I settled into a routine. On a Thursday, everyone's afternoon off, I used to go round to my nan's on the way home from work, as I knew that Dad would be there having his dinner and I would have a bite as well. Nan used to save me some and then I would walk home with Dad and I would prepare the tea for the others and do his sandwiches for his pack up. It was the one afternoon where he could be free and not worry about the meal. I also used to do my washing on Thursday afternoons, the bigger items which you could not just rinse out and get dried overnight.

Tuesday and Thursday nights, used to be hair wash and mend night and *Top of the Pops* used to come on. A new music program where all the new number one in the chart songs would be sung by the groups, that's the only time I ever saw the Beatles playing, the one I liked the best was Paul McCartney, he was far the handsomest.

I used to get the *Jackie* comic, although I had to give Dad the money to pay for it, being about sixpence at the time. It used to give you a poster in it now and again and they had one of Michael Landon, who played Little Joe in Bonanza, he was my pin up, I never saw him in much after Bonanza. I suppose he was in stuff but he never surfaced to me until *Little House on the Prairie*. He was still a handsome devil.

One thing that I really hated at work was the fact that on some dinner times I was left to run the counter and it was, as I said, very long. It was at twelve o'clock when a load of yanks would come in (Americans from the R.A.F bases at Coltishall). They were out to make me blush, I always felt tongue-tied. They would come to the electrical end of the big, long counter near the cash office and ask for bulbs, cable etc. and when they gave me the money they would put it into my palm and drag their middle finger down my palm and my fingers and it used to make my skin crawl and obviously I blushed.

When I handed the change back, I would make sure that they did not get hold of my hand. When I told Lou about this, she told me that it was a sexual thing, so it made me even more aware of them. Most of them must have been in their thirties, which was old for me then and I had been asked to go out with a few of them for a cup of coffee, in their American drawl, at that time I would never have thought about going out with an older man. Most of them would go to the American Club, which I believe was on the Salhouse Road and my sister Christine had been there once or twice.

Mr Linley used to think he was a comedian and was constantly cracking jokes, which I suppose was better than being an ogre. He must have been in his late thirties; he did not have any grey hair, which I associated with an older person. Anyway, after I had been there a bit, whenever I left off and would be walking to the front door, he would call me back the full length of that wooden floor and I would say, "Yes what did you want?"

He would reply, "How far would you have been if I hadn't called you back?"

Well we were taught to respect our elders and I would not have dared to be rude about it. This went on for quite a while and in the end I told my dad and he said to me, "You will have to tell him next time he does it."

So the next time he did it, I went back and I said to him, "This is the last time that I will be coming back from the door when you call, as you want nothing important." I then turned around and walked quickly out, relieved, to say the least. He did do it the next night and I just kept on walking, then it stopped.

Lou, the lady who I was put with to learn the ropes, when she found out that my mother had died young, she said, "If there is anything you need to know about anything just ask."

Well that time came sooner than expected. As I have told you, I was a very naïve for a fifteen year old and I have said that I walked into work, I used to come down Philadelphia Lane, along Angel Road and then St. .Augustine's. As I neared St Augustine's swimming pool, a boy on the other side of the road said to me, "Give us a wank." I just smiled and carried on walking, when I got to work, I took Lou aside and said, "You know you said I could ask you anything well, what's a wank?"

Lou said, "You're not serious are you?" I explained what had happened and she then told me what it was and I was aghast, and I will tell you why. My dad when he got angry with us sometimes used to say, "You kids aren't worth a wank."

The next time Dad said it, I said to him, "You must not say that as it is rude and not nice." I never heard him say it again as I now knew what it meant. I'm surprised that Dad did not ask me how I knew.

Yvonne and I started to go to the Melody Rooms on a Friday night, it used to be called the Industrial Club and it was on Oak Street, it is now called *The Talk of The East*. It was one and six to get in and we only had a shandy, as we weren't allowed to have alcohol. To actually get out, was like running the gauntlet in our house. I used to practically run home and get me tea, have a quick wash and change out of my work clothes, as I used to have going out clothes, and wouldn't wear what I had been to work in to go out, like Sunday best. I learnt this practice from Christine, her going out clothes were always good and she had a few suits in which she looked like a model.

As there was Robert and Jeannette in the house, I did not put make-up on, I did not have any at that time and would charge out of the house before John and David did, and run up the road so no one could catch me to stay in and look after them.

Wasn't I an awful sister? Jeanette had a panic attack once and I was not there to help her out. I did feel a bit guilty but I had to go out sometimes didn't I?

Yvonne was never ready, she would lend me her make-up and she would do my eyes. At that time the little spidery look was all in and she did it really well but she stopped doing it for me because she said I looked better than her, not that I minded as it was a compliment. I eventually bought some make-up from Woolworth's. A blue and green eye shadow, a pale pink lipstick and like a hard powder in stick form and a black mascara, but not the spit and brush one, like my sisters used. It's a wonder they didn't end up with eye complaints from their own spit as you should really have used water but as we did not have a bathroom upstairs when they were getting ready, they made do with spit.

As I said, Yvonne now worked for Lambert's on Ber Street and she had started to smoke, when we used to go on the dance floor she said to me, "Have a cigarette, it will set your hands off." Have you ever heard of such a stupid thing? This is where I tried my first cigarette and I did not like it.

The only thing to do at the nightclub was to walk round and round the edges of the dance floor and through the bar area, we always went early as it was cheaper, after ten the price went up. I preferred the Samson but I could not always get in there as I was underage and I looked it, on a Monday they used to do a teenager night.

When walking round, you could see who was there and on one of these walkabouts, a boy came up to me and asked if I would come and sit down with him to talk, so Yvonne went to talk to some people we knew and I went to sit down. He had white overalls on and had come to the disco straight from work, he had dark hair and a pleasant face, the next thing I knew he kissed me, my first proper kiss and I did not like it, he put his tongue down my throat. I ran to the ladies' cloak room and stayed in there. Yvonne came in and said, "What's going on? He's just asked me to come and see if you are all right."

I said, "I don't want to go out with him and I'm not coming out of here until he's gone, can you get rid of him for me?" So she did, that poor man he went home but he was not actually dressed to come in a place like that. I hoped that all kissing wasn't like that but maybe I did not know him well enough.

We used to walk home along Angel Road and then Catton Grove Road, maybe get some fish and chips; we could get a lot for our money in those days. If I had been a mean person, I could have walked up Philadelphia Lane and through George Pope Road, which would have been a lot quicker for me but I did not like to see her walk alone and there was always safety in numbers.

We would walk up Woodcock Road hill and then part company at the top of the hill, at Bullard Road, as she lived on Middleton Close just off Harmer Road and Saffron Square.

When Yvonne went her way I would get my tail ended steel comb out of my pocket and keep it in my hand, as it was very dark walking along Bullard Road and my sister Christine had been accosted by a man with his penis out, so she never went that way again in the dark.

Christmas came and I bought presents for all the family and Nan, from Woolworth's of course, it was wonderful being able to do this and I remember buying some thick jumpers for everyone and all sorts of bits and pieces. I had bought myself, in the time from July to December, two twinsets of all things, but they were classic pieces to everyone's wardrobe. a pink one and a blue one. I also bought two nylon bras, no underwires (I don't think they existed then), they had rosebuds on them, and knickers to match, one black and white and one red and white set, size thirty two A. I just about had put on another half inch up top.

I also bought clothes from a catalogue and had got a navy skirt, sort of A line but swishy material and I matched it with a blue short sleeved blouse in a soft material and an emerald green cardigan. I know they say that green and blue should never be seen together, but it did work. I had bought a pair of navy shoes in a shop in St. Augustine's, as they did smaller sizes and as I was only a two and a half shoe, they had a decent heel on them so I could walk alright and they were toes and back out. I had a brown skirt the same and a pink blouse to go with it and I think I had some tan coloured shoes that had a sponge like sole to wear with them, not high heels but a clumpier heel. I think they were a pair that I had from school. When I wore my black polo neck, it used to make my bust look bigger, I had always wanted to have bigger breasts but they do say be careful what you wish for, as later in life I got them and I really do not like them.

March 1969, Yvonne told me that they had a vacancy as a junior in the office where she worked, although it was not in the same department, did I want to see if she could get me an interview. I jumped at the chance, as I did not really like working in the shop. I got an interview for two thirty on the Thursday afternoon. I was really nervous, the interview was with a Mr Smith, no not related to Yvonne, there is just a lot of Smiths about. He was a short, kindly man who put you at ease straight away and asked me a few questions about myself and I did not do any tests at all. I was told that the job consisted of filing, going to the post, getting pies for his elevenses at the bakery near the post office; I laughed when he said that, and general dogsbody. He told me there and then that I had the job and could start Monday week at five pounds a week, an extra ten shillings a week, fantastic.

My dad was really pleased with me because office work was a prestige job then and it had the bonus of having more wages.

Friday morning, I had to give Mr Linley the letter that I had written and he said he would miss me as I was a good worker and he would give me a good reference, so that done I duly left on the next Saturday.

I could barely breathe with the excitement that weekend. Me in an office!

Monday came and I bussed to work and went in at the back entrance

Lambert's was a family run business and I went in and up the back stairs, turned left and the ladies cloakroom was the first door, so I went in and took my coat off, then went out into the corridor again. The next door on the left was the kitchen where you could have your break and dinnertime sandwiches.

On down the corridor, and the next office on the left is where the typing pool was, such as it was, it consisted of two girls, Carol and Pauline, I always thought that these two looked like models in their suntans and good clothes. Pauline always used to drive without any shoes on in the summer and used to wear Scholls, which were wooden sandals with leather tops, in the office.

A room going off that was where the new accounts were made up and where there was a machine to print multiple letters, it had a roll drum and a handle which you turned but it was not a photocopier. They did not have one of them. Eileen was responsible for that room.

The door opposite was the room where I would be.

On the right hand side, was where all the pigeonholes were, it would be my job to put the morning post into the appropriate boxes. At quarter to four, I would have to empty them of the letters that had to be sent out and would frank them all then take them over to the post office.

Then into the office where I would be working, on the left hand side of the room were the N.R.C machines, these machines put the money owing on to peoples accounts from the invoices that the sales reps would bring in every day after they had been on their travels. Mr. Smith looked at these before they went onto the accounts. There were five of these machines with the manager of them being Doreen Taylor, a lady in her forties, her husband was the Lord Mayor of Norwich's chauffer.

On the right side of this was where I would be, with Miss Rose who did the accounts, she was a thin lady who wore glasses, she was a spinster in her late fifties. Mr. Smith's desk was in front of the frosted glass window that divided the next room off. The franking machine was on a desk quite close to Mr. Smith's that was so he could see no one abused it for their own letters. On the wall, there were loads of shelves with invoices on them and there were loads of invoices, for filing, on the two tables where I would be sitting.

Through the other door, there was an office on the left, where the lady wages clerk sat and there was a man called Vivien Sumner in that room as well. In the main room, sat Yvonne on her comptometer I still don't understand what exactly it did. There was a Mr Russell and another two ladies in there. I feel awful that I can't remember all the names of the people that I have worked with over the years but it has been thirty-four years and the old brain won't work like it used to.

Out of that room, into the corridor and on the left hand side, was the personal secretary of the managing director, her name was Phillipa Irene Pippen and of course they called her Pip, she was a middle aged lady always on a diet, something that I thought I would never have to do.

The next room was the managing director's room and he always brought his dog in with him, a great big Golden Labrador, he was a nice old thing but I was still very wary of dogs.

Out of his room, to the door at the top of the front stairs, that led down to the reception area. The phones consisted of the ones that had headphones and wired plugs that you put into the right connection and the girl who did it was so quick I used to think she was marvellous.

The reception consisted of chairs and a coffee table.

There was a door that led into the warehouse and there seemed to be loads of people that worked there, even a married couple. There were all the shelves of cigarettes and sweets and you got a small discount off them. The warehouse people would get an invoice and get the goods up and they would go in plastic crate-like baskets and be taken along on rollers and into the transport department where the men would load up on the appropriate vans that would then take them out to places like Dereham etc. They had a great big scale there and it was one that I had to use if I ever had any really huge parcels to take over to the post.

Then out of that door and you came to the back stairs, up those and on the left hand side at the top, was another director and his name was Mr Raynor, he was an elderly gentleman, polite and quite a joker

To the right of his room, further up the corridor was the storeroom where all the old accounts and stationary was kept.

If you went back down the corridor, nearly opposite the kitchen was another door, behind it was an empty room, really dark and you crossed the floorboards and came into another department where a Mr Rose was situated (not related to Miss Rose). He was so handsome in a craggy face sort of a way, (I did like Charles Bronson), he was in his forties and he was head of the tea mixing and tasting, they also did the Ninhams cake mix there. I had to go through there every day to collect his post as he always said he did not do his letters until as late as possible. So there ended the introduction to my new work place.

I was taught how to use the franking machine and shown where the post office was, I had to go across Finklegate and *The New Inn* pub was opposite that road, where many a dinnertime was spent at Christmas time. Then across the crossing to the post office, next to the bakery where I had to go every morning at ten o'clock.

I quickly got stuck into the filing and the day went really quickly, I loved it. Yvonne and I caught the bus home together, we walked to Upper King Street to catch it, which is called Tombland and I got off at Philadelphia Lane, as it was closest to me.

Yvonne and I went to the disco that Friday night and I met a boy called Gordon, he had lovely blond hair and blue eyes, he lived at Poringland, he kissed quite nice, better than my first one. Yvonne copped off with his mate and they decided to walk us home. We parted at Bullard Road and at the end of Bullard Road and the corner of Jewson Road was a big hedge and we lolled against this and he put his hand up my top and I said, "Don't do that, I'm not like that."

He said, "Look, I've walked all this way and I need a little something."

"Well you won't be getting that little something from me," I replied.

"I'm going then," he said.

"Bye then, mind how you go," I said, then I went home. Yvonne got a date for Saturday night, but I don't think he turned up.

We sometimes used to go up to the bowling alley on a Saturday afternoon, not always to play, as we couldn't afford it, we had to have a coffee in there, but it was a meeting place for some of the teenagers and several of the older blokes. I think Yvonne fancied one of them; it was lovely having all my Saturdays off.

Even then walking up Magdalena Street after four o clock in the dark, a rainmac man came in the opposite direction and gave me a flash. What is it with me and flashers? Apparently this man was well known for it.

Yvonne always had short hair and she used to wear leather coats all the time, which she got from her brother's stall. So I thought I had better get me a new coat. My nan came with me to a shop in Davey Place, in the middle of the city and I bought a turquoise blue, swing back, it had like purse-clasp metal things to do up. Although I thought it was wonderful at the time, I felt too conspicuous when I saw what the other girls were wearing, most of them wore dark colours, but I liked bright colours, and still do. I tried to buy one new item of clothing once a month, things were not cheap like they are now.

Dad used to have a man come round on a Saturday, Mr Taylor was his name, and he used to bring clothes round, which you could buy on tick. If there was something that you needed he would try to find it for you. The first thing that I bought off him was a navy pair of women's Chelsea boots. They were leather with gusseted sides, very comfortable and I wore them with a pair of boy's Levis jeans. These originated from America so that is probably why they cost me about £26.00, a lot of money. I had to save up for three months to buy them, and I actually had to buy them at a shop in Davey Place as they did not have a pair small enough on the market, which is where most people got theirs. I had to get a size twenty-eight inch waist so that they would fit on my hips, so the waist was too big but the hips fitted, as most women have got bigger hips than men and obviously, a short leg. These were worn with a boy's checked shirt. I had a blue and white one and a brown and white, they had patterned neckerchiefs to match, one blue and one brown. I thought I looked wonderful and very modern and I did feel part of the scene at that time. I have still got the blue neckerchief, I found it the other day when having a clear out, there are some things you like to hang on to. Dad used to say, "Why have you got that thing round your neck. Take it off and let me look." He thought I was wearing it to cover up a love bite. Moi? He must be joking. He used to do this as regularly as clockwork, only to the girls of course. Still the only time I did have one he never looked, how lucky was I?

He always wore leather boots with side zips in them, never anything like a sandal, heaven forbid, only hippies wore such things. You had to laugh at him, bless him. Mind you, when I saw a photograph of him after he had been abroad with John, his little, thin, white chicken legs in shorts were hilarious, he never wore shorts at home, I can understand why.

Anyway, one night when I was wearing these very things, I went as usual to the Melody Rooms with Yvonne and right in the back room which was kept well lit. I came across my brother Stephen's mate, Billy, (don't know why they call him Billy I thought his name was Richard). Anyhow, he was likable enough and he said he would give us a lift home as he lived across the way from Yvonne, (Billy must be a bit older than my Stephen as he obviously had a licence to drive). Anyway, he dropped Yvonne off first instead of me and we sat in his van, I believe he did kiss me but I did not fancy him sexually. He eventually took me home and the next week my brother Stephen said Billy told him that I had had sex with him and I told him that I had not and I never spoke to Billy from then on.

In later years, he has been to many of our family parties. He obviously noticed that I was a bit off with him whenever we met and he asked Christine, not me the person he should have asked, why did I not speak to him. Christine asked me why I did not like him and I told her what Stephen had said, she then told Billy next time she saw him and he, when next he saw me, denied saying it to Stephen and I said, "Why would Stephen make up such a story?" So, whether he confronted Stephen with it I do not know but Stephen has never said anything else to me about it, as I denied it at the time and it still stands.

I do talk to Billy when I see him now but I always feel very uncomfortable around him. Still, all the rest of the family seems to get on with him OK, so perhaps it's just me being silly.

Stephen had another friend called Barry B, who was tall dark and handsome, that old cliché. I fancied him like anything but he was too young for me. Stephen used to bring him home, usually on a Sunday just as it was dinnertime, perhaps he never got fed at home but I would take a little from everyone's plate and there were plenty of batters, so he got fed. I'm sure that Barry knew that I had a fancy for him as I was a blusher. As he got older, he took the look of Brian Ferry with those smouldering eyes that were quite a turn on, although later on, when I got older, he would take that as an insult because he would say that Brian Ferry was ugly.

*

So, back to the workplace and my first encounter with the warehouse crew. I suppose it was a sort of initiation, I went down to take the orders to the woman in charge, and when I went out, back through where they loaded the basket-like skips/crates on to the lorries. They scuffed me up and dumped me into an empty skip, then dumped it onto the rollers and it shot off into the back of one of the vans because, as I have said before, I was very tiny and did not weigh much. I was a bit scared but they were all laughing, so when I got out, I laughed as well, although I felt terribly embarrassed, blushing like crazy and girls were not allowed to wear trousers at that time, not in the office anyhow. I had stockings on which got laddered, tights at that time were very expensive as they were a new invention for everyday wear.

I had to go into the ladies' to wash my hands and brush myself down. I had to go to the secretaries to see if they had any nail varnish as I had never worn it and I knew that they did, they all laughed when I told them about what had happened. That was my initiation.

I loved working at Lambert's but I never seemed to have as much as the other girls for lunch, I sometimes took a couple slices of bread and an Oxo cube, so it was like having soup, or I would buy a small tin of beans to have on the two slices of bread, toasted.

Lyndsey was a woman who worked on one of the N.C.R. machines and had a lot of sandwiches for lunch she had them in greaseproof paper. They were doorsteps but she was thin and she only ever ate three, she would give me the other one, when I finally let my pride take them. I think that I could have eaten for England. I was forever hungry.

She did not have any children and I believe she was in her thirties, she had to put drops in her eyes three times a day as she had no tear ducts, she hated it that when she had a row with her husband, she could not cry.

Lindsey's husband would collect her at the end of the workday, and if they were going my way home, along the Aylsham Road, they would give me a lift which would save a bit of money on bus fare.

He was one of those know-alls and he was a bit of a bully and a control freak. They had a big black car: I think it was foreign. I saw her in an office that I went to in my thirties, she had divorced her husband and she had had a child and she looked really happy. Good for her.

I was nearing my sixteenth birthday and everyone kept saying wasn't I excited and I told them that I wouldn't get much anyhow, Dad never bought birthday presents. All the office workers clubbed together and presented me with a sum of money to go and blow on what I wanted; it was tremendous thing to do as they had not known me long. Yvonne and I went to Bonds on the Friday dinnertime, as we had an hour for lunch, it is now called John Lewis, they had a shoe sale on and I bought a pair of three-inch navy sandals size three, a navy bag and some perfume. One called Tweed, which I know people think was an older ladies perfume but I liked it and thought it was classy, and one called Electrique by Max Factor, which was more of a teenage perfume. I used to wear the Tweed for work and Electrique for going out. I came back with my purchases and they all liked what I had bought.

This outfit that I have got on is pink lace with a pink bra-slip underneath it and as you can see I had it buttoned up to the top. I had my three-inch navy sandals on, or I wouldn't have looked that tall. Christine had put my hair up. As you can see I hated smiling, I have an awful smile, it just never looks right. It was on this day I believe I walked down the road and Mr Brandish whistled at me. Apparently, he said to my dad, "Your girls walk down the street as if they owned it."

Me at sixteen and Christine, outside the gate of 42 Jewson road. We must have been going to a wedding as we both have flowers on our lapels.

My dad replied, "They do, don't they?"

Dad always said that we were to hold our heads up high and we did.

My sister Christine taught me how to walk tall, and often put the broom handle up the back of me and told me to walk with it, I must admit it certainly made me walk straight. Hence I always look taller than I am. Even when I'm in my car I have the seat upright and the seat really forward. (It's because I cannot reach the pedals really).

On the way home one Friday night, as I have said before I used to walk up to the top of Woodcock Road with Yvonne and turn off at Bullard Road. As I was walking, I felt that there was someone behind me, so I slid my steel comb out of my jeans pocket and into my hand so I had some protection. Then I crossed the road and ran the rest of the way. I ran in through the back door and John was there, I said, "I think someone was following me."

He ran out but came back and said no one was there. Well a month went by and it happened again but I got a look at him this time as I crossed over the road but I did not speak to him. I saw him standing outside of a house at the top of the hill; I now knew what he looked like.

Another month went by and it happened again but as I crossed the road, and he did as well, we came to the phone box and I swung round with my comb in my hand and looked really shocked, I said "Why do you keep following me?"

He said, "I want to ask you to go out with me."

I said, "Why could you not do that in the daylight?"

He did not give me an answer so I said, "Well, if you think I would go out with a stalker, you had better think again and I know where you live so if it happens again I will be straight into this phone box and on to the police."

He still followed me and I ran up the road and John again came out with the poker in his hand but he said he did not see anyone. That was the last time that it happened but I did come home a different way now and again and I never saw him again.

I met a lad called Alan P at The Melody Rooms, he had short blond hair and was pretty. He worked at Bonds in the scenery and price signs, which he painted, he actually wanted to be a window dresser. They had a studio in All Saints Green and I often used to visit him in my dinnertime.

He would come and collect me from home and we would walk down the road and people would whistle at him as he used to wear a pink, fluffy coat and platform shoes and I would feel embarrassed as they were definitely whistling at him. He kissed alright and always treated me with affection but he was a bit effeminate. I just stopped going out with him as people used to laugh at him and I could not handle it.

1970 was here and I was loving work, they had employed another girl in my department and her name was Yvonne S, can you believe it? But they called her by her second name, which was Gloria. I think that she was part-time and we sometimes used to go back to her flat for lunch.

She had quite a pock marked face, she covered this in a thick pan stick. The powder, she must have got through one a week how thick she trowelled it on. She had a nice figure and her skirts were really short. She was a good worker.

I was still doing baby-sitting for my aunts and when they did not want me on a Friday or Saturday, I would be at The Melody Rooms, in fact I went there on a Friday, Saturday, Sunday Monday and Wednesday. Tuesday and Thursdays would be washing your hair night, and washing and ironing all the things that you had not had time to do.

So, as usual on a Friday, me and Yvonne were at The Melody Rooms. I saw this really nice boy as we were walking round. He was standing with his mate, Roy, and Pamela M, who lived up the road from me. She was slightly older than me and had long, wiry, ginger hair, quite good looking and I did not know her well. Pamela came up to me and asked me to come over as Glen liked the look of me and wanted to be my boyfriend, so I told Yvonne and went over.

Glen was not tall but everyone is usually tall to me, he had dark hair and a twinkle in his eye. He was a few years older than me. We did kiss on that first night and it was the best kiss I had had up to date. He did put his tongue in my mouth and I must have liked it that time but he moaned about a sharp tooth I have and I said that if he did not like it, not to put his tongue in my mouth but he still did.

Anyhow, that started a great friendship with Pamela and we sort of stayed as a foursome going down to Hemsby in Roy's Mini occasionally,

It was a bit cold for the beach. We sometimes went onto Mousehold Heath at night and ran the peeping toms about, putting them in the headlights. The things we teenagers did. I had been going out with Glen for about six weeks and Saturday 21st March, the Eurovision contest was on, so we all went round to Roy's to watch it as his parent's had gone out. Well we did watch, it was in Amsterdam and Ireland came first with *All Kinds of Everything* sung by Dana .We came second that year with *Knock Knock* sung by Mary Hopkins. We had a heavy petting session and Glen took me upstairs as Pam and Roy were going to as well. We went into a bedroom with a single bed in it and continued petting and then the moment came, he put on a condom and inserted his penis in. I made a little scream as it hurt and he said, "My God, you are a virgin."

I said, "What made you think I wasn't?"

He replied, "I thought you were just a prick-tease, I have never had sex with a virgin before, do you still want to continue?"

I said, "There is a first time for everything and this is my turn." So we continued and after that first hurt, it was OK and I had finally turned on my sexuality.

Going home that night, we went in Roy's Mini and we were in the back, it was getting quite late, they stopped outside my house, and who should be coming down the road but my dad? I can picture it now, the fear that went into my face as he came over to the door and he actually dragged Pam out of her seat. He had her by the arms and she was shouting, "Mr Rowell, Mr Rowell, it's me, Mr Rowell it's Pam, stop shaking me."

"Sorry but you should be in as well this time of night," Dad said. I was out of the car by then and I was frightened and embarrassed at the same time, the boys stayed in the car (they did not get out of the car to protect us) Pam got in and they went up the road to Pam's.

"What the hell are you playing at being home this late?" shouted Dad, at this time he had grabbed hold of me by the waist of my jeans and I was practically horizontal, as I have said I was a lightweight and he broke the zip on my precious Levis.

I broke away from him and said, "I hate you." Then I ran as fast as I could into the outside toilet, locked the door and bawled my eyes out.

My dad came to the door a little while afterwards and said, "You had better come in now as it is cold out there and I want to lock up."

I said, "You aren't going to hit me are you?"

He replied, "No I've had enough embarrassment for one night."

So I came out and he kissed me goodnight, I said, "I don't really hate you but I was just so embarrassed. What am I going to say to Pam?"

He said, "She will forgive me if she is really your friend and a good girl, not like her older sister who's had three babies with different fathers." He said what he always said. "Once is a mistake. Twice is stupid. Three times is just downright irresponsible."

God almighty I thought, a good job he did not know what I just had been up to. Pam never did tell me if she had done it with Roy that night.

I went to Pam's on the Sunday and she said, "We were okay and the boy's thought it was hilarious." And she found someone that would put a new zip in my jeans but they never looked the same to me after that.

I don't know that Glen had his own Mini but we did go out in a different one. Once we went down onto a boat, which one of his friends had, through nettles and long grass, where we had sex, as once I had started it was nice but we never did it in a bed again. At least I can say I did not lose my virginity in the back of a car.

We petered out after a while and for some reason Pamela had stopped going out with Roy, so instead of going out with Yvonne, who had then started to go out with Michael S, Pamela and I knocked about together until I got married. I have never seen Glen since then but Roy did jump on a bus one Easter when I was going home from work and he gave me a bottle of Babycham that he had won on the Easter Fair, which was on the bus route and then he jumped off the bus.

The term prick-tease, I had heard it a few times before and this was from boyfriends with whom I had not indulged with the heavy petting, as I used to go out with a different boy once a month. I suppose once I had ensnared a boy I had been eyeing up, I lost interest in them. I never thought about a bad reputation at that time but I knew I was not having sex with them.

Why is it OK anyhow, for boys to do it anytime they like and not get called names but a girl can lose her good name and get called slag, slut and tart?

Men always have it all and I sometimes wish that I had been born a man rather than a woman, as men seemed to have much more freedom and get away with so much more.

My stepsister to be, Diane, was a wee bit older than me and braver. She used to go down the Melody Rooms when the bands were playing and I used to get frightened for her. I suppose she was a bit of an adventurer (or a groupie), this might be a bit of a shock to her family, she used to go backstage to see the groups and, later, she would get in the back of the roadies' vans with some other girls and be taken to parties that they had afterwards. If I saw her doing this, I would go over the road to her house the next day and make sure that she had got home safely without Ruby, her mum, knowing why I was asking. I used to ask if Diane wanted to come out for a walk on the park or something like that or that I wanted her opinion on something.

All the family liked Diane she always had short hair and she was really thin, she did have two bigger teeth at the front but not goofy as we used to call it.

Unfortunately, Diane died two months before her fiftieth birthday, she just died in the lounge of Dad's flat, in front of my dad and Ruby, for no apparent reason. Dad held her hand until the ambulance men came but it was too late from the time that she had hit the floor. Poor Ruby had, just eighteen months before that, lost Paul before his fiftieth birthday as well, although he had a few medical problems, it is still unexpected to die before your parents, he just dropped dead in *Ketts Tavern* public house, so at least he was in a place that he wanted to be. He used to be manager of the *Beehive* public house in Sprowston, Norwich. Before he got worse for wear, God bless him. How strange that two of Ruby's children died just before their fiftieth birthdays.

Ruby never got over these deaths as no one expects their children to die before you do and she went steadily downhill.

Pamela had a friend who was having an eighteenth, all-night, birthday party, and she wanted to know if we could bring some boys. I cannot remember how the H twins came in to the picture; they were both cute at that time, one quieter than the other. Kenneth and Keith were their names and I still don't know which one took me. They were proper Mods and you didn't have to wear helmets in those days.

Getting to go to an all-night party was traumatic and never done for the girls to stay out all night. Well I went to Ruby over the road to see if she could sweet talk to him before I asked him, crafty was I not? I did ask him, and he said yes and told me to make sure I behaved myself.

Saturday night came and the boys came to collect us, it was great being on the back of a scooter, better than getting a taxi. We didn't take any booze with us and it was very quiet when we got there, hardly anyone there, so the boys got stuck into the beer and got merry. Later on, a few more people came and the music got a bit louder. I have never been so bored and from about ten o'clock I wanted to go home. There were people all up the stairs, kissing and doing heavy petting, so it was a job to get up to the toilet.

Well, after twelve o clock people started to leave but we stayed, as the twins could not ride their scooters, they had had too much to drink. The twin I was with, and me, got on the couch and had a kiss and a cuddle and although he tried to have sex with me I did not want to. I think that I had got myself a bit stressed out and I had a headache and a stomach ache. I thought I had better get to the toilet which I did and I had got my period so I asked Pam if she had something with her as mine was not due, she did and she introduced me to Lillets, a smaller tampon which I could manage to insert all right.

I came downstairs and my twin asked me if I was all right and I had to tell him that I had got my period. I often wonder whether he believed me. We stayed on the couch and about five o'clock we decided to go home, we told Pam and her twin we were going and they came too. Got dropped off at my house and all was quiet and so the toilet came in handy once again. I did not dare to wake up the house. About six-thirty, Dad came down to the toilet and got a shock to see me sitting there. He said, "Why did you not wake me up to let you in?"

"You don't get much of a lie in so I did not want to make all that noise, if I had a key I could let myself in,"

"You won't get a key until you are eighteen."

I went in and got my sanitary things, cleaned myself up and went to bed for a few hours.

I have seen the H twins over the years and still remain friends, in fact I saw one of them when I went swimming the other day and I just say hello, not naming him as I still don't know which is which and they are not so cute now, but haven't we all changed.

My brother, David, was always asking me to go out with his friends and said, "John B asked me to ask you if you would go out with him on a date?"

John B lived around the corner from us; he was a stocky lad with a mullet haircut. "I don't really like him as boyfriend material."

"Please, just go out with him the once, be kind."

"OK, but I do so under protest."

Around he came on his scooter and I think we went on the park, I did not know what to say to him, that's if we spoke at all.

We went back home and he tried to kiss me and to let him down gently, I did that old thing, it's not you me it's me I'm not ready for a boyfriend. Then I went indoors.

I said to David, "Please do not try to set me up with any more of your friends as I like to pick out my own." David was not too pleased but he never asked me again.

My Sunday treat, since I had been working, was to go out to Mr Deans lorry, yes he had graduated from the horse and cart. It was great that he came round on a Sunday, if you had run out of anything and wanted a fresh vegetable he was very handy as the shops were not open and a lot of women bought potatoes so they did not have to carry them home from the shops. He came between twelve and twelve thirty and I would buy half a pound of grapes if they were in season, a bag of salt and vinegar crisps and a mars bar. Pure luxury.

I sometimes gave Jeannette some grapes but I did not share them often.

What I did do, so Jeannette occasionally had a few coins, was ask her to clear my handbag out and that she could have all the change smaller than a shilling (that's twelve old pennies), if she found any. I did purposely leave some in the bottom of the bag, as she never had pocket money; none of us did after Mum died.

*

I went out with a boy on our street called Victor, I say went out but we never really went anywhere as he always had his head under a car and we occasionally went out in the country and did a bit of heavy petting. He invited me to be his guest at his sister's wedding reception, it was at the labour club and when I went, I sat with his mum all night. How could he do that? I was distraught and crying, he had obviously dumped me so to speak. Christine was sleeping in my room at the time and she said, "Stop crying, you keep making the covers shake," so I got out of bed onto the floor, pulled the eiderdown on top of me and cried away.

"Do you feel better now?" she said.

"You know that it's still happened and you will have red eyes in the morning and will look as if you cared, it wasn't as if you were in love with him." She was right, as usual, I wasn't in love with him but it was so embarrassing. Why did he ask me if he knew he was going to dump me? His sister had even done my hair that morning. Still as Christine says, it's his loss and she was right.

*

I met another chap down the Melody Rooms, as I was not old enough to go into pubs. His name was Ronnie G, he was a bit older than me and I liked him a lot, he used to leave me at the club as he had to get up early in the mornings, he worked on the buses and did early shifts. He had a friend who was always trying to break us up. I believe that my brother John was working on the buses at that time and he warned me off him as only brothers do. Of course I paid him no attention, in fact it made me want him even more. I didn't like to take people round home as it always smelt like cheesy feet with all the boys feet. Ronnie actually did make it to the house but it was short and sweet as I got him out of there double quick.

Ronnie was an ex-army man in his twenties and had a scar down his cheek which made him more interesting.

Ronnie was separated from his wife, not yet divorced, and he lived in a bedsit that was on Grovesnor Road. I went there several times and we had sex in his single bed and it was like an explosion had happened to my insides the first time that we had sex, as that is what it was to me. Ronnie gave me my first orgasm, it was fantastic, he moaned a lot and I said, "What's up, doc?"

He said, "That was unbelievable." Then we did it some more, he was very sensitive man for an ex-army man.

He cooked good meals on his little oven but the only thing was that the loo and bathroom were out in the corridor, making it hard to clean yourself up. At this time I was not using condoms so it was a wonder I did not get pregnant. Before I had sex with him, we did talk of other partners we had had, in my case only one at that time, but he convinced me he was free from anything. It was nice being with an older man, and he took me to tea at his sister's. She lived in the Towers on the Heartsease Estate, we of course had to catch a bus as he did not have his own transport but it cost him nothing. I must have made a good impression on his sister as Ronnie kept telling me she liked me.

I was still going out and about with Pamela at this time. We used to go out into the city on a Saturday and she introduced me to the shop account. She had one at Fifth Avenue, so I got myself one and I bought a herringbone greenie-grey coat with a mini hemline and a grey, wool, herringbone pinafore dress with a zip all the way down the back, which could be worn with or without a blouse/jumper under it. These were the only things that I bought from this shop as it was a very expensive and I paid it up as soon as possible. I did buy a little red dress with small bunches of flowers on it and a peter pan collar, but it was dry clean only and I went and washed it, it shrunk so I had to give it to Jeannette as it went that small.

Ronnie never had a lot of money as he was paying maintenance to his wife and his children, so we often used to meet up at the Melody Rooms. One particular night, the Ryan Twins were on stage with, I'm sure, a backing group called The People but I could be wrong. The Ryan twins were so handsome; they harmonised wonderfully and were my favourite singers at that time. I was watching them singing and Ronnie came and found me. He took me to one side and said, "My wife is here I did not know that she was coming, I think she has come to get a look at you."

"Well I'm not leaving. I've paid my money and I'm staying here with Yvonne." (I think I had gone with her that night).

"You know that I will be leaving at ten as I have got to get up in the morning, just be careful."

He left and the Ryan Twins had finished singing, I dare not go backstage to get their autographs so Yvonne got it for me, they were fabulous. As the years have gone by, I lost my autograph book; I don't think that it would have been worth much today. Anyway, I was walking around the floor and his wife came up to me and said, "You are going out with me husband." Then she promptly punched me on the nose. I was shocked. My nose was bleeding so I quickly went to the ladies cloakroom, when I saw the red blood I went ballistic. You've got to remember, I was a bit of a mouse, still very tiny. I went charging out of the ladies and went into the bar area of the club. There she was, leaning against a cigarette machine and laughing with a friend of hers and that made me even madder. Well, I gave her an uppercut, knocked her off her feet, then she sort of went slowly down the wall and I just dived on her, punching at her. It took four bouncers to get me off her, they told me to go back to the ladies' cloakroom. The strength you find when you are really mad is frightening at times.

My pinafore zip had come undone so I was showing everything off, good job I had clean underwear on. Yvonne zipped me up and took me back. I was cleaning up in the toilets and his wife jumped on my back again the bouncers came in, took her off my back and chucked her out of the club as they said she was a known troublemaker. That was my one and only fight.

When I was walking home, I stopped at the phone box on my road and phoned Ronnie to tell him what had happened and he said, "I've got a revolver. I'll go round and sort her out." (The revolver was one that his father had given him from the war.)

I said, "Don't be so daft, that wouldn't do your divorce case any good and you wouldn't be able to see your children."

"You're right," he said, "I think she realises just how much I like you and in fact I want to marry you. You will then have the same name as my mum."

I said, "See you on Sunday afternoon."

I went home and slept on it with my bright red nose. I did not know what to think.

He met me outside Debenhams, where all the bus stops were, and we walked back to his bedsit and he told me his wife had phoned up and said that she was really frightened of me, that's a laugh, little ole me.

I was into the musical *Hair* at that time. When we went back to his place, I wanted to play the LP on his record player but he would not let me as he was in a bad mood so I said, "If you think that I am marrying you, you've got another thing coming." I duly smashed the record over his head, got my things together and walked out of the door.

That was the end of that little interlude. I did not even cry as I had left him on my own terms and I did not love him, although the sex was good.

Brother John was pleased that I had stopped going out with him. John said, "He was way too old for you." Still I was only seventeen and I had had my first proposal, although not a romantic one.

I have seen Ronnie three times in all this while and he always says, "What's up, Doc?" I still blush like crazy.

*

At work, life went on and I had progressed to the N.C. R machines, they were very heavy machines and went clunk, clunk as they went along on the cogs, it was only part time at first so I could learn how to do this job. I was still doing the post at that time as well. One Friday afternoon I went over to the post-office to get the insurance stamps as usual, when I came back I did not have one of the more expensive ones. I had to go back to the post-office and they said that they could do nothing until Monday when they would have tallied up the stamps that they had left. So that left me all weekend to stew in my own juice and if they had not got it at the post-office I would have to pay for another one out of my own wages.

That Friday night, I had to go babysit at my Aunt Pat's and Uncle Dennis', so I went to catch the bus at the bottom of Philadelphia Lane. Alan, the boy next door to where I lived, was waiting for a bus. He was quite handsome in a boyish way, I blushed as usual and he said, "Cheer up, it might not ever happen."

"It already has," I said. I then proceeded to tell him about the stamp and he was very kind and listened to me, then he asked me to go out with him the next night and I said yes.

That Saturday night, Alan picked me up outside my gate. We walked to St. Augustine's Street and I got my introduction to pubs, although I was underage. I kept a low profile when Alan went to buy the drinks, so the first pub I ever went into was *The Chrome*, just before where the *Odeon* picture house was at that time. The pub had a quirky little gas cigarette lighter on a long thin arm that went around over the top of the bar and I was most amused by it, so the smokers at least didn't have to buy matches. I tried a port and lemon and it became my drink for a while. I always thought it was a classy drink and it was sweet enough for my sweet tooth. Another pub we went in, was *The Cat and The Fiddle* in Magdelen Street, which has also closed down. Then we went up to the *Artichoke*, on the corner of Bull Close and Magdelen Road, making our way back home so we went in a circle. We then on to what he called his local, *The Lacon Arms*, where his friends used to drink, a couple that he saw most of all were Trevor and June; they were most friendly and took to me straight away. When I got to know the crowd in there, they used to say I was an only child, there was a laugh and I said, "Why do you think that I am an only child?"

Laughing with Alan as they said it, "Cause you talk nice and you are quiet and good mannered, not like us little lot." Then I told them that I was from a family of ten and they wouldn't believe it 'til Alan told them that it was true and that he lived next door.

June used to work at the supermarket on Aylsham Road, which is now Barclays Bank. June was a pretty girl and they were engaged and were getting married the next year.

Back to the Monday after that Saturday night. I went back to the post office and it turned out that they had not given me the particular stamp that I had had on my list on the previous Friday, as I always handed the list over and it had not been torn from their pad although they had ticked it off my list. Thank God for that, so that was one catastrophe averted and not taken out of my wages. So, Alan was right, it did not happen.

Now and then, Alan used to borrow his dad's car and when we came home, we would have sex in the back of it, inside the garage at the top of our road. We used condoms and he used to throw them on the dump as we went past, all wrapped up in tissues, it's a dirty old job but somebody has to do it as they say. It was nice sex, not as passionate as what I had had with Ronnie but it was OK. I know that I had to scrub myself and used Dettol (which I kept in my bedroom so no one else could use it.), to calm down the itching as I was allergic to rubber if you can remember and I don't think they had any other sort of condoms at that particular time. My little halfpenny must have been the cleanest one on the street. Sometimes we would lock the back door and the stair door so no-one could get into the lounge at my house and do it on the carpet in front of the fire, that was very nice. Stephen used to protest about this and would bang on the stair door to be let in. "I know what you are up to!" But you had to do what you had to do in those days and not when Dad was likely to come home, so weekends were out. I suppose I was quite naughty really but I was growing up fast however tiny I was.

At work there started to be changes; they got a junior in to do the post, as they wanted me to be full time on the N.C.R machine, which I loved. I cannot remember what the girl's name was and she kept telling me how to do the job when I was supposed to be showing her. I helped her out now and again. I know I once got so angry with her that when she started telling me what to do again, I said, "Just drop dead and shut up why don't you." That very weekend, she was run over by a bus. I was mortified and have never wished anyone dead since. It certainly taught me a lesson, as I had to do the job until they got someone else in.

Another thing happened with a new person, it was a new secretary who had come to take the place of Pauline, who had left to have a baby. Her name was Joanna, I can picture her now. She had crinkly, ginger hair and enormous glasses, she had a very nice figure and used to wear her skirts short and buttons undone far too low for work in my estimation. Well the managing director's son had come to learn the job and he took a fancy to Joanna, who was engaged at the time but it did not deter her, the man was short, blond haired and blue eyed and he also wore glasses but the funny thing was that they thought no-one knew about them.

We had got the auditors in. It was Kevin W from school, the one that I had fancied, he used the managing director's office on the right of the stairs, near the stock cupboard. As I had been doing the filing, I knew where everything in the cupboard. That particular day he wanted some old invoices, I went in the cupboard with a list and went about to find them. One of them was right at the top of the shelves, so I clambered up and sat at the back looking at the invoices and the next minute, Joanna, the secretary and the director's son came tumbling into the room, kissing like anything. I did not say a word and I thought if they get into anything too passionate, then I will speak to let them know I am here, then a call came out for him and he said, "I'll meet you dinnertime, usual place, I'll go out first and you wait a bit then follow."

"OK," she said, she then proceeded to get some notebooks for her dictation and some corrector ink and went out, how they did not notice me I did not have a clue but I know it was a relief to get down and stretch my legs.

I finished what I was doing and took the invoices to Kevin and he said, "You were a long time."

"I couldn't find one of the really old ones." My explanation anyhow. When I had finished with Kevin, I thought, do I tell them that I had seen them, or not, that is the question. My answer to my own question was yes, as they could then be a bit more discreet. So, I asked Joanna if she could help me in the ladies for a moment and

I said, "I was in the store cupboard when you both came tumbling in."

She was really shocked. "Why did you not speak?"

"I was way too embarrassed to say anything and had you gone any further than kissing I would have had to speak or cough."

"You won't tell anyone else will you? I'll probably lose my job if you do."

I told her that I would not say anything but that I believed everyone had an inkling about it anyhow.

I think that it took a couple of months to dwindle out after the director's son moved to another of the branches but I never did tell, until now.

One night as I left work at five o clock, I got as far as the repair garage, I was about to step off the kerb when a car turned in the road and the man in the car said, "How much?"

Me, not being streetwise, as they would say today, said, "Pardon, did you want directions?"

"I said, how much is it?"

"How much is what?"

"For a blow job?"

I actually knew what one of them was now.

"I'm not a prostitute!"

"Will you do it anyhow?"

I do not swear but I said, "Fuck off," and walked round the side of the car to continue my way home. Bloody kerb crawlers that time of the evening. I do not know why he thought I was one of them I did not wear my skirts too short or tight or my tops too revealing, not for work. I was not amused.

It was getting near Christmas and I had bought a turquoise, high necked blouse with a black bow on the front and buttons down the back, very Edwardian, and a long black skirt from C and A. I already had the patent shoes with a buckle on the front, bought from C and A, it was a new store in the city at that time, which boasted of good prices and they were.

Alan and I are right at the far end of the table.

I did not notice it before but the first lady on the left hand side looks like Hilda Ogden out of *Coronation Street*. The first man on the right taught me to waltz; he was supposed to be a bit of a ladies' man.

I was very excited as we were going to *The Norwood Rooms* for the Christmas party, held the last week in January as we could not get in before and I actually had someone to take with me, I went on my own the year before.

The day of the wedding of June and Trevor was coming up and I had to find something to wear and of course good old C and A came up trumps. I bought a lilac, midi outfit that had a calf length button through skirt and a waistcoat. I bought a shade darker, lilac, leg of mutton sleeved blouse that had little buttons on the side and I bought some shoes, off Mr Taylor, that had crossed straps on them and buttons, in a sort of burgundy/maroon colour, matched perfectly, so I had got that sorted.

Two weeks before the wedding, a very peculiar thing happened, I got a phone call at work from Trevor, and he wanted to see me. I told him I would meet him after work but what was all the secrecy and he said I would find out when I saw him. He must have got the phone number of my work place out of the phone book as I had never given him the number and he knew where I worked. I thought it was maybe he wanted me to do something for June, his fiancée. I said before, I was a bit naïve, even at seventeen, where boys were concerned and I would never learn.

I got in the car and I said, "What's it all about then?"

"You know I've always fancied you." Then he tried to kiss me.

"Have you gone mad? You are getting married in a couple of weeks' time."

"I don't know whether I want to get married."

"This is something you should be discussing with June and I am not going to be your last fling. Whatever would she say if she knew that you had come on to your friend's girlfriend?"

"You aren't going to tell her are you?"

"No I won't. I'll put it down to wedding nerves and don't do anything like it again. Now you are here you can give me a lift home as you have made me miss my bus."

So he took me as far as Jet Alley and I walked the rest of the way home. Thinking about it, this was not the first time that someone's fiancée, had come on to me. I must give out the wrong vibes for them to think that I would do something behind a friend's back like that.

It happened when I went out with Gloria (the second Yvonne at my place of work), there used to be a diner on the cattle market, near the Castle, which was next to where they used to have the fair at Christmas and Easter. The diner was like an American one that I had seen in pictures and on the TV. Gloria and I used to meet the clan there on occasions and then we would go to the *Rouen* pub and get the landlady to open the back room where we could be as rowdy as we liked. It smelt of cats and we often used to find cold cat's shit in there, it had like sitting room chairs in it. Well this particular night, there was a handsome chap amongst the boys and I liked him a lot, he was single, a lot older than me and a biker, he gave me a little sterling silver ring but he was very quiet and did not want any girlfriends, he always got very drunk. Anyhow it got a bit late and I had to get home, I think the buses stopped running at ten-thirty at that time and Gloria's fiancé said, "I'll walk you home."

I said, "It's too far."

But he insisted and I said my goodnights and we started walking to my home, just chatting in general and we got as far as Waterloo Park, Angel Road side, and he got hold of me and said, "I deserve something for walking you home."

I said, "I didn't ask you to."

He tried kissing me, breathing hard he said, "Give me a wank?"

"Not bloody likely," I practically shouted back.

I believe I slapped his face and said, "You had better be getting back to Gloria as she will wonder why you're taking so long."

Then off he went and I walked home at a faster pace than we had been doing.

I never said anything to Gloria but I made sure I was never on my own with him again.

Anyhow I digress, back to the situation with Trevor, I told Alan that I did not want to go to the wedding and he obviously asked me why and so I told him what Trevor had done and he said, "I don't believe it."

"Why would I make up something like that?"

"You'll have to go to the wedding or they will think something is the matter."

"Something is the matter and he will know anyhow. I'll feel really uncomfortable."

"Please come as I will feel silly and I won't be able to tell them why you aren't there." So we went to the wedding and it was a lovely day and they had the reception at The Manor House on Drayton Road, (it is now a Lidl's supermarket). I can't remember which church they got married in.

I had had a midi haircut and Jeannette had her hair cut the same, I thought I looked wonderful and so did the photographer. He asked me if I would model for him as I had good bone structure, he had a place on Magdalen Street. He gave me his card, I never did take him up on the offer as you heard so many strange things about photographers and their studios. These things that happen can make a girl very stand-offish to people, if you have to be on your guard all the time, and Alan still did not believe that Trevor, his mate, had come on to me.

Alan was made redundant from his job at the window place in Colgate and we did not go out much. I remember that I bought him a whole new outfit from Mr Taylor for his birthday, even down to a new pair of brown boots, I also bought him two shirts, one a peachy colour and a blue one and they had matching kipper ties. I did not buy him trousers, as they were a bit too intimate to buy for him. All my life, I have been one of life's givers and I get immense pleasure from it.

I am actually smiling in this photograph
and it does not look too bad

I got him to mend the broken window of my little bedroom as there was a draught coming in and he did a few more, so at least the house looked better with new panes in them.

My feelings gradually waned from Alan; it was the fact that he did not believe me over the Trevor matter and the thought of his distrust in me. I kept with him until the right time came to tell him.

That summer, me, Pam, her sister Andrea and a girl whose father played in the band at *The Norwood Rooms*, I believe his last name was Cooper, went on a caravan holiday down to Hemsby.

Andrea, Andrea's Friend, Pam, Me and Cooper

Andrea's friend had gate crashed on us and we couldn't really say no.

Cooper's dad took us down there in his van so we did not have to pay bus fares. I had to pay my board as usual for that week as my dad said, "Your bed is still there." What could I say, although the other girls didn't have to pay for theirs. Life is not always fair is it?

I had got a couple of new dresses for the holiday, both shirt style as that style in dresses seemed to suit me better, one bright yellow and one turquoise, which I bought in a boutique in Norwich, size ten, when I went out in the yellow one that holiday, it covered in greenfly. It was very hot that summer. The dress I have on in the photo came out of Pam's catalogue and was made of nylon, very cheap it was and as you can see I put a big hem on it.

When we were down there we met this group of Scottish boys and they were on our caravan site. There was one particular one called Alex, who I thought was pretty damn gorgeous. They came to our caravan one afternoon and were talking about music, they liked the way T. Rex played and said they could make that sound and, believe you me, they did, with the pots and pans as instruments. As usual, I embarrassed myself as I had my period. I think it was the stress of doing something new again as I had never had a holiday away. I went to the cupboard to find something, and my packet of Lillets fell out and some rolled onto the floor, good job they were individually wrapped as one of the boys picked one up and said, "Whatever sort of cigarette is this?" I blushed of course, and had to grab it from him, so they knew they were mine. They just laughed and did not say anything else about it. We decided that we would all go skinny dipping that night at midnight, we were up for it and although we did not actually skinny dip, as the water was too damn cold, we went in with our jeans on and in the morning there were five pairs of jeans hanging out of the windows to dry.

Alex and I hit it off and talked a lot about family and during the week, the boys decided to stay some in their caravan with three of the girls and Pam and I were in ours, me with Alex and Pam with another of the boys.

We did sleep together, it was nice to cuddle and he wanted to have sex with me but I had my period didn't I? He still wanted to do it but I just couldn't, it did not seem right to me.

Next day in the morning I threw up and Pam said, "You're not pregnant, are you?"

"Don't be daft I've got my period haven't I."

"It has been known for woman to still have a period and be pregnant."

That was something I never knew until Pam told me, you seem to learn something every day in life.

We said goodbye to the boys and Cooper's dad came to pick us up and we all went to our various abodes, it was nice to be home in my own bed.

*

Pam used to come round the house on maybe Tuesdays and Thursdays. I still kept these nights as not going out and she had a portable record player, which you could put records in, she used to make us laugh as she would put my brother's big steel capped boots on and dance about, can you imagine it, her little thin legs in these great big boots.

She actually had a hair dryer, which is one of the reasons she came round, so I could dry my hair, she was a great mate who earned a bit more money than me. She also used to iron her's straight because, as I have told you, it was ginger and crinkly, she would put it on the board and put brown paper on top of it, it did work, we did not have the tongs to straighten hair then.

Talking of record players, my brother Stephen was now at work at a shoe factory in Colgate, which is now one of The Norwich Union buildings (Aviva). He had got hold of a second-hand record player and it was in a suitcase looking case. He had two records at that time, one of them was *Candy Girl* by the Allsorts, he would play this record time and time again. It was doing my head in and I wanted to watch something on the telly so I went to turn it off and I suddenly got this kick from behind with the toe of the boot hitting my fanny (not bum). My God, the pain was excruciating and my breath was taken away, I suppose it must have been a bit like a man getting hit in the balls. What is it with these boys, I always seem to get hurt down there and Stephen had no remorse. I cried out with the pain and hobbled to the kitchen to get some cold water to ease it. It did not bleed but it did blow up a bit with the bruise.

I did not tell Dad as Stephen definitely would have felt the touch of the old persuader. Stephen probably doesn't remember the incident but people often choose to forget when they have been cruel.

*

A couple of weeks went by and although I went out with Alan, things were a bit strained, and his brother was getting married, of course I was supposed to be going to the wedding.

I went up the road to Pam's on that Saturday of the wedding and Andrea was there and she said, "I have got something for you."

"What's that then?"

"A letter from Alex as you couldn't give him your address."

"I didn't give him my address as he lived to far away to be in a relationship."

She gave me the letter and I read it, he was saying how much he had enjoyed meeting me, he was a little older than me, hoped that I did not mind him writing via Andrea and would I please write him back him at the address on the letter and there were kisses on the bottom.

I put the letter in my back pocket and went home to get ready for the wedding and who came out into the passage as I was going in, but Alan. He put his arms around me and went to kiss me, his hands went down my back to where the letter was and he pulled it out of my pocket and said, "What's this?"

I took it out of his hand and said, "Just a letter from a friend."

"What sort of friend?"

"Just someone I met on holiday."

I don't know what was said next but I know I tore the letter up in front of him so he could not read it. He then said, "I told Trevor and June that I was going to ask you to marry me at the wedding."

"No good telling them was it? I've been back two weeks and we have not been right have we? And you obviously don't trust me and don't believe what I say." We had been going downhill since Trevor and June's wedding, to the extent that he was not even happy with what I was wearing, like a nice white straight dress with a tie belt, I was wearing it with a white bra-slip underneath it and he said it was too see-through. God, it was the 1970s. It's the same old story; he liked that sort of thing on other girls but not on his own girlfriend.

Mind you, it brought to mind something else my dad used to say. "You might as well go out in one of my vests."

"Have you got one I can use?"

"You cheeky monkey."

We did get away with a bit more these days, as I suppose Ruby kept him up to date with things, having three daughters of her own.

Anyhow, that is when we broke up and he said, "You will never find someone who loves you like I do." That was the only time that he had told me he loved me. I did not go to the wedding. Why are men so vain as to think that no one could love me enough to want to marry me? How wrong was he? That was my second marriage proposal. I never discussed past boyfriends with him as I do not think it is a good base for a good relationship, as it stokes the jealous streak.

Anyway, there went another one of mine and again I did not cry as we broke up on my terms.

As Alan lived next door to me, we couldn't really avoid one another and when he used to come down the road late at night, he would whistle the same tune over and over again but I cannot think what one it was but I sometimes would peep out of the window and he would be looking up. The whistling would last as long as I lived there.

*

When I had two weeks holiday, usually around my birthday as I have never worked on my birthday, I would go up to see Christine in Richmond. I was quite brave, I used to go up on the train and she would meet me at the station then we would catch another train to Thames Ditton. Christine had Monica at that time, she had a job at the dentist's surgery, and I would go into the village and meet her. She must have had Monica in childcare, as I know she was not with her when I went to meet her. Anyhow, I was walking along the road, in my brown hot-pants, pink t shirt, long, pink, knitted cardigan and my tight burgundy boots and to my amazement a white sports car drove up to me with a beautiful blond man in it.

He asked me, did I want to be a model on a photo shoot as I was just what they were looking for.

"What, as the before photo?"

He laughed and said, "No, definitely the after."

As I said before, I am not a very brave person and I just said, "No."

Another lost opportunity maybe, as that was now two similar offers that I had had but I did not think that I was particularly beautiful but perhaps I could have been another Twiggy.

I did tell Christine and she said that I had done the right thing.

I had bought myself a wet-look bikini, which came out of Pam's catalogue, it had like shorts' bottoms with a belt and silver buttons on it and it was a thirty-four bust. I weighed seven and half stone and I was five foot. So I had grown a bit, out as well as up and I did think that I looked very well in this bikini. Christine took me to her local swimming baths, which had an inside swimming pool which took you to an outside one with grass around the sides and from the looks I was getting, the boys thought I looked good too. It does your ego good.

Christine and Millis, took me out to one of their regular pubs to have a drink. I was still underage at this time in 1971, and in this particular bar was a band of brass musicians having a drink after music practice. This one guy kept looking at me and I smiled at him, he did not come and ask me if I wanted to go out with him but asked Millis the next time he went to the bar and gave him his phone number so I could ring him the next day if I wanted to, his name was Brian.

I duly rang him from Christine's the next day, he arranged to pick me up and we went to his work place as he worked on the pumps at a garage near Wimbledon, where he lived. I even had a go on the pumps, filling a car up; it was an experience for later on in life. He drove a Mini of course.

I always seem to pick people who have not got much money and he wanted me to come up to his, so I said to him that I would come up every fortnight as I could not afford it every week. He used to ring me at the phone box at a certain time a couple of times a week to stay in touch with me. So I stayed with Christine a few times and one of those times he took me to Little Hampton and we were kissing and he wanted a blowjob.

"What here?"

"Yes it makes it more exciting doing it somewhere that you shouldn't."

We were in the car on the sea front.

So I did, but I was no good at that, I was no good at hand jobs either.

And of course we got the coach load of holiday makers go past and he thought it was hilarious, I didn't, I was so embarrassed.

"Don't be silly, you will never see them again will you? They probably got the thrill of their lives and they never saw your face did they?"

I felt awful sponging off Christine when I came up and said to Brian, "I don't think that I should come up as often."

He said that I could stay at his as he lived with his mum and they had a spare room for guests, so I said OK.

Stephen had his record player in an old small brown case, so I took his record player out so I could use it as a weekend case. Good thinking, I did not want him to think that I had nothing to put my stuff in, as I had used a carrier bag before. Getting on the train to Thames Ditton was a bit nerve racking, sometimes if it was crowded, you would get a man sitting next to you. They always sat with their knees at an angle and if they were a bit pervy, they would put their hands on their thighs right next to yours and rub their fingers up and down. Many a time I have gotten off my seat and stood, rather than put up with it.

The next Friday night, I stayed at his. I took my little case and when he saw it he laughed at it. He took me to band practice with him and I met his fellow mates in the band and one couple that he was friendlier with than the others. He introduced me to them but I'm blowed if I can remember their names, and they were engaged. On the Saturday, the band was playing at Bellevue (I thought it was called the Rose Bowl) at the stock car racing.

They called him a cradle snatcher as I was not even eighteen and he was in his twenties. I had my port and lemon as usual, as I wasn't really allowed to drink. I've always thought that it was very unfair that you could go to work at fifteen and pay your taxes and N.H.S. stamp but not to be able to drink or get married without an older person's permission.

I went to his house to sleep and in the morning, I woke up as he snuck into my room. "What are you doing here?" I do ask stupid questions don't I?

"I just wanted to cuddle you."

"What if your mother hears you are in the room with me?"

"She has gone out so I thought I would sneak in."

He was in the nude and he had the smallest penis I had seen up to date.

I had not had intercourse with him yet and I did not want to start now but I was saved by his mother's key in the door and he went down to make me some breakfast and then we had to get ready to go to catch the coach.

I had brought with me a pair of cream trousers and blue tunic, long jacket, to wear and yes, you guessed, as in all times of stress, I got my period when it was not due. I had to wear the jacket in the coach all the time, as it had come through onto my trousers, as I saw when I went into the ladies' at a stop. I had to buy some at the station as I did not bring any with me, all through my life I have had this thing in times of stress of something new to me. I did not tell Brian but I did tell his mate's girlfriend.

When we reached the hotel, which was at Bellevue they had booked me and Brian into a double room and the engaged couple into two singles. I was mortified but I was saved again by the engaged couple asking if they could exchange with us and I said that I did not mind but Brian was not too pleased.

We watched the stock car racing, it was very exciting and I enjoyed it very much. The brass band played at the interval and that was quite pleasant too.

We had a nice meal and went to a pub and then to bed to our separate rooms. I got undressed and then Brian knocked on the door, my room had a little sink in it so I had my sanitary stuff on it. I told him that he could only have a kiss goodnight as I had got a period. I don't think he believed me so I told him to ask his mate's girlfriend and I think he did as he did not pester me anymore.

We got back on the coach the next day, it was Sunday and I had to go to catch my train back to Norwich. I usually walked back home from the train station to save a bit of money as well as not having to hang about waiting for the infrequent Sunday service.

The next time I went down to London, I stayed with Christine. Brian took me into town, he kept looking in jeweller's windows and he said, "Would I like a nice engagement ring for birthday?"

I assume that that was a proposal of marriage and I said

"I would rather have a nice weekend case as you laughed at the one that I was using."

So he bought me a weekend case, light tan in colour, with a vanity mirror in and everything and I was very pleased.

Brian thought that it was about time that he met my dad, so we arranged that he would come down the weekend of my birthday. I had not wanted him to come down as I had said before, the house was not best for visitors. He was to come down in his Mini on the Thursday afternoon and I started my holiday on Friday, so I could be with him awhile and my birthday was on the Saturday, my eighteenth. On the Thursday night when I got home from work, I asked Dad where he was and he said that he was over Ruby's having a cup of tea and then he said, "When are you getting married?"

"I'm not."

"Well he seems to think that you are and he told me he was going to marry you, he was asking my permission and is coming down to Norwich to live as the job scene looks better here than in London."

"Well I will have to put him right won't I?"

"Tell him gently, as he seems to care for you."

I just didn't find him sexually attractive and just couldn't do it with him, it had nothing to do with the size of his penis.

Brian was sleeping in my bed, at the back down the long corridor and I was in bed with Jeannette. I thought I had better go to him and sort him out. I got in bed with my dressing gown on and said to him, "I hear you told my dad that you were going to marry me. I don't remember accepting a ring."

"You didn't but I still thought…"

"I am not ready to settle down with anyone and I think it would be better if we split up." (The old it's me not you.). Then I got up and went back to the other room...

When I got up the next morning he was gone, it was for the best.

I believe that he did come down to Norwich to live and I saw him once, and he had a perm, but we did not speak.

*

The day of my eighteenth birthday came. Dad had bought me a brown and cream umbrella, as I had not got a decent one of my own, some cheeky underwear that Ruby had chosen for me and I got a petticoat and tights from my nan, as they were now a bit cheaper than they used to be and better under the shorter skirts, and I got a key to the door. The voting age had now changed from twenty-one to eighteen so I could now vote in the next election.

Now I was eighteen, I could officially go into the pubs. There was one on Aylsham Road called the *Edward VII,* and they started to have music with a D.J. spinning the records, Pam and I went in there a few times. One night I met a boy called Glenn in there, he was quite tall and dark and had a quiet nature. He liked the speedway and he lived on the Heartsease Estate on Deloney Road, with his mum and small brother.

His mum used to go to what we would call grab a grannie night, at the *Samson and Hercules* dancehall at Tombland, opposite Norwich Cathedral, and we would have to look after his brother. If we wanted to go to the speedway on a Wednesday in Kings Lynn, we would have to take him with us. His brother was a little sod, very annoying.

The smell of the speedway was intoxicating and the excitement always filled the air, the danger of it all was exhilarating and would last you until the next time you went. Glenn had a white Ford Anglia, his pride and joy; he would pick me up outside my house whenever we went anywhere, in style.

We went occasionally to a few nightclubs but mainly it was a pub, Glenn did not drink much as I think he did not want to be like his dad. We did not do any heavy petting and he was another person who was more like a brother than a boyfriend.

One night near Christmas, December the 11th to be exact, was the date that I met my husband, Brian. I was in the pub with Glenn and while he was in the toilet, I was trying to get to the bar and this boy walked past. As I said before, I was short. He had one of those sheepskin waistcoats that Sonny out of Sonny and Cher had made popular (*I've got you Babe*). He had a bit of fur sticking up on the top of the sleeve and it went right under my nose so that's how we started to talk. He said, "Sorry about that, who are you with?"

Glenn had just come out of the toilet and I said, "Him," pointing to Glenn coming out of the toilet.

"Oh! That loser."

Typical male remark. Anyhow, Glenn had come back to me by then. "Who's that you are talking to?"

Here goes I thought, same old jealous crap.

"I don't know who he is," and then I told him about the fur going up my nose and he was just saying sorry.

"Trying to pick you up more like."

"Well he did not succeed did he? Or I would not be standing here with you getting the third degree."

Of course, the night was ruined, we ended up having a row and I ditched him there and then, after he had taken me home of course. I cannot stand being accused of something that I have not done.

After Christmas, Pam and I had gone to the *Edward*, on a Friday night again, and there was Brian up the corner of the bar, apparently it was his assigned place and he stood nowhere else. He had long hair which curled at the ends and he was about five six .He said, "Hello, nice to see you again," he spoke quietly and very posh like.

The *Edward* had two rooms at that time, the other room had all the lights on and was for the older generation, then Brian said, "If you are staying in this pub you might want to go in the other room as there will be some Hells Angels in here later and they are looking for trouble."

"Okay, thanks."

So Pam and I went into the other room and the Hells Angels came in; we could see through from the other room. The Landlady (Francis) at the time, had one of the Hells Angels in a stranglehold over the top of the bar, she was pretty awesome to watch, there was glass everywhere then everything went quiet. The landlord, it was rumoured, had tried to commit suicide by hanging a rope over the wood beams of the bar, put it around his neck and proceeded to jump off the bar but the rope was too long and all he did was to sprain his ankles, daft old sod.

Brian then came through to us and said we could go back into the other room if we wanted to.

"Are you still going out with that boy?"

"No I'm not."

"Would you like to go and see the new James Bond film at the Odeon?"

"I would love to."

We then decided to meet at the beginning of Anglia Square, as it would be better for the both of us. He could not drive, he was only seven months older than me, his birthday was 16th December and he worked at Panks Engineering on Castle Hill, which is now a model shop (cars, planes etc).

Pam had met this boy at her workplace, which I believe was called Diamond and H, you'll have to forgive me if that is wrong but it has been a while, I know it was quite a well-paid job in their office. She arranged to go out with him that Friday so we both had dates.

Friday duly came and I tried to eat my tea, which was my favourite, shepherd's pie, and as usual I put it in sandwiches and Dad said, "I might as well make you sandwiches instead of slaving over a hot stove all afternoon." I cracked up because he sounded just as a woman would sound.

"Dad I'm in a hurry, I'm going to the pictures and they start really early, about half six."

"Watch what you're up to on the back row."

"Dad… I will be watching the film no 'hanky panky' when it costs a lot of money."

"Enjoy it then."

Then he got his lunch box to go to work, he still worked nights at B.R.S.

I was as nervous as anything. I had put my pinafore dress on and my herringbone coat with plain, baggy, black boots, most of my boots were baggy as my legs were really thin and my brothers used to say I had lucky legs, lucky they held me up, or when I had my brown platforms on, they would call me Minnie Mouse.

He stood waiting in Anglia Square as arranged, he looked very smart in a jacket and trousers and he took my arm and we walked to the picture house, we chatted on the way and I found out that he had gone to the Hewitt School and he knew of my brother John.

The film was *Diamonds are Forever*, it came out in 1971 but had only just come to Norwich, the queues were massive and went all the way down the steps and down into Anglia Square, which had not long been finished. There was a Purdy's burger joint on the corner, very American. The old *Odeon* had been pulled down to make way for the new. The Bond film was full so we went to see *Monty Pythons Flying Circus*, which was a comedy made from episodes from the television series of the same title.

We did not sit on back row, no overtures were made to me and we thoroughly enjoyed the film, we did laugh but who wouldn't?

He duly walked me home and we did kiss and I thought, this is nice, and we made arrangements to see each other again the next Saturday .We only went to the *Edward* for a drink that night. On the Sunday, as his sister, Carol had just had a baby, he wanted me to go with him to the hospital and see them both. I thought it was a bit soon to meet the family but he seemed to be all right about it. Of course his parents were there and Brian's mum introduced herself as she said, "If I leave it to Brian it would never happen."

I put my foot in it when I saw the baby and I said "It's all yellow."

I was, as I said, a bit naïve and it apparently had jaundice.

After that, Brian took me to his house to meet his mum and dad properly, as she had told him to bring me back for tea. His mum was called Becky, not christened Rebecca, and his dad, Bert short for Bertram. She was very nice and said, "I can see why he has been getting his body up in the evenings now."

His father, I was very unsure about.

They had a white poodle and it yapped and yapped, when I went out the door to leave, it bit me on the back of my leg but it didn't leave a mark as I had trousers on, thank goodness.

His father said, "It will let you in but it won't let you out."

I told Brian I would not go round his house again unless the dog was put out of the way and it always was after that. We had arranged to go out the next Saturday.

The next Saturday came and we went to the pub next to where he worked and I met a workmate called Richard, and his girlfriend, they were nice and she came from a well-off family and was an only child, used to getting her own way with anything and everything and she ruled Richard with an iron fist.

The weeks went by and I grew to have feelings for Brian that I had never really felt with anyone else. One night Brian had walked me up to the top of Jet Alley near the garages, and we were kissing and my dad walked past and he said, "Is that you, Jo?" I think he asked because he did not want to get it wrong after the Pam incident.

"Yes, Dad."

"I expect you indoors in the next ten minutes."

"OK, Dad."

So we quickly kissed again and said goodnight and I went tearing down the road and indoors right sharpish.

"You shouldn't really be doing courting there."

"I know, but it is better there than doing kissing in front of the gate."

One evening, we went out to the *Edward*, we met another of Brian's friends called Paul and his fiancée called Janice, she was very exotic looking but she was as English as me. She had long, black hair, an olive skin and a lovely figure and we got on very well, we are still great friends to this day, she had been going out with Paul since she was fourteen.

I had also met his mate, Peter, who was in the landscape business; he was then going out with a girl who was an au pair. She was a tall, long legged blonde, a very typical bimbo, she did not seem to have a lot of common sense, also another of his friends who was of Meatloaf proportions and he had a big motorbike and a great big silver car.

Brian and I only went out at the weekends and one Friday he rang me up at my workplace and said, "Don't be alarmed when you see me," he had broken his foot and had it in plaster.

When I asked how he had done it, he said, "We were playing football in the yard dinnertime and I fell down a small drain where the lid had fell off."

The thought of suing anyone in those days never entered our heads, as they shouldn't have been playing football in the yard.

I told him that I would come round to his house to pick him up if he still wanted to go out, although he was on painkillers and could not drink, he insisted that he would meet me at the end of the road as usual.

When I got to him, he was laughing like hell.

"What's tickled you?"

"I was looking down the road near the kerb to see if you were coming up the road and an old lady escorted me across the road, even though I did not need to cross but she insisted, so I let her. I then had to wait till she was out of sight before crossing back over which took ages."

His foot mended but it would always be weak and I don't think that he would have ever been a footballer to start with.

We started to go round his mum's after we had been out and we would do some heavy petting before he walked me home. You could say that Brian was quite the gentleman. One night I had been drinking gin and orange, I had just changed my drink from port and lemon as it seemed a more grown up drink. I was really drunk and I begged him to make love to me, we had been seeing each other for three months at this time and we had talked of me going on the pill as I was allergic to the rubber of the condoms and had itching and a bit of a swelling after I had used them. We had done nothing but heavy petting up until then, not that that was not good but not as satisfying as the real thing. He said, "No, you're too drunk and I will not take advantage of you in that condition."

Spoilsport, but he was right wasn't he? I think I fell a little more for him because of that.

On the Sunday, his parents had gone out for the afternoon and wouldn't be back till late, we got worked up and only made it to the settee, not even to his bedroom where it would have been a bit more private and he had a condom. It was fantastic but (of course there is a but) the condom had split, I know people say it does not happen but it does and it did.

I should have had my period the next week but as you can guess, it did not happen and I knew that I was pregnant, even at a few days gone without anyone having to tell me.

Easter Sunday was the christening of his sister's new baby, Jason, and I had got an outfit out of the catalogue, it was a pink and white check dress with a white jacket, I wore my navy shoes with them. It was only the second time I had seen his sister and she made me welcome, at the eats afterwards, she said, "When are you two tying the knot? This has been the longest Brian has ever been out with a girl."

I replied, "It might be sooner than you think."

The day passed, I had a lot on my mind and the next morning I found a small pill bottle, peed into it and wrapped it in a brown paper bag as there was a chemist on Gentleman's Walk that did pregnancy testing. I told Yvonne and she said she would come down to the chemist with me in the dinnertime. It was very expensive to have the testing done, it cost me ten shillings, I'd wanted it done within the hour, which I did and had to borrow money off Yvonne and pay her back on the Friday.

We went and bought chips off the market, as that was opposite the chemists, then I went to collect the results as they could have it done within the hour and I dare not open it so Yvonne opened it for me.

"Are you ready?"

"I know it really but it is just confirmation."

"You are officially pregnant,"

It was still a shock, even though I knew, I felt sick for the rest of the day.

That weekend, I did the usual things to get rid of it, I was that desperate not to be pregnant, Brian did not know at that time.

Gin and a boiling hot bath, what a load of twaddle, all you got was a scalded bum and fanny.

Then to this day, I do not know what possessed me (desperation) but I put a knitting needle up. I could have punctured anything, not just damaging the foetus and I cried and cried to think what I could have done and had to face up to the inevitable and to my responsibilities, the next thing was to tell Brian. It was just meant to be.

I went to the doctor's on the Wednesday night, as you did not have to make appointments in those days, you just went up to reception desk and told them who you were and you just waited in the waiting room as they called you.

I told the doctor that I was pregnant and he said, "That is silly of you, have you told your dad yet?"

"No, I haven't plucked up the courage yet. I wasn't being irresponsible, (I don't think that he believed me), the condom broke."

Doctor said, "The best form of contraception is not to do it at all." He felt my tummy, made sure I was all right and said, "I can't do anything about it if you can have it, as you have not got any illnesses and you are perfectly well enough to have it and look after it."

I had not told the doctor what I had done to try to get rid of it, so I had just come to the doctor's to be on his books that I was pregnant.

I came out of the doctors feeling very small and told off.

I had arranged to go up to my sister, Christine's, in Richmond, as she had just had her second baby and I was going up to help out. Robert had come home by that time so there was a bit more room.

I told Christine and she said, "I never thought you would end up in the same position as I had been in."

"I did not think I would either, but I have and now I have to tell Brian."

"You haven't told him yet?"

"I had to get my own head round it first, I suppose we will get married."

"Tell Ruby before you tell Dad." That's what I did.

We did not speak of it for the rest of the week and I got my hand in changing nappies and feeding the little one.

The first person I told after that was my nan, and she said, "Do you want me to tell your dad?"

"No, I'm going to get Ruby to tell him."

Nan gave me £10 to put towards the wedding and that was her present, a very good sum of money in those days. I always went to see my nan at least once a week and one week after I had spoken to my dad, I went to see my nan. She had my dad's younger brother, Albert, staying with her, after being chucked out again from his home, a very arrogant man and an ego as big as it could be, when he heard that I was pregnant he said, "You've made your bed and you must lie on it."

I still don't really know why he made that sort of comment, but I do know, that whenever he spoke to me again, it really makes you wonder why.

I went home and then I had to speak to Brian, we stayed in his house to have the chat and when I told him he said, "I suppose we had better get married then."

"Not if you don't want to, I do not want you marrying me to leave me soon after, just because I am pregnant I know it's not the ideal way to start a marriage."

"I would not do that, I suppose I had better go see your dad."

"I haven't told him yet I'll let you know when I do."

Then off I went to tell Ruby and she said, "He won't be very pleased but I did it for Christine, so I can do it for you."

Ruby apparently said, "You cannot condemn your daughter when you had to get married yourself."

I went home and waited for the storm to start but it didn't, as I have said, Ruby seemed to know what to say to Dad.

"When is Jesus coming to see me?"

Dad was talking about Brian with his long hair, he didn't wear sandals, but he did wear wide-leg jeans. We arranged for them to meet in the *Windmill* pub on Aylsham Road, Dad seemed OK with him and he knew his parents, as they came in the pub at weekends, so I did not really have to introduce them as he would probably see them anyhow.

Brian told me later that Dad had said, "If you ever harm my girl in any way, you will have me to answer to."

The next thing to do was to get a date and see the registrar at City Hall, as we would not be able to afford a church wedding. We both took an early lunch, as the City Hall was shut at dinner times. We gave the registrar our details and paid the fee, which I think was £1-10 shillings, we had decided on the third of June, a month off my nineteenth birthday and I would not be showing too much.

At this time, I had grown another three inches in height and was now five feet and weighed seven stone eleven, I had about six weeks to sort out where we were going to live, where we were holding the reception, who was coming, what I was going to wear etc. etc.

I had twenty-five pounds to my name saved up and Brian had about the same. On the Saturday we went out to buy the rings and bought them at *The Gold Shop* on Gentleman's Walk. I bought Brian's, which was a plain band and he bought me a cut band it was very pretty. His plain band was more expensive than mine, even though mine had more work on it.

The next thing I had to do was get a cake and I asked our bakery delivery guy if they did wedding cakes, he gave me a little brochure and I ordered a two tier horseshoe shaped one, it cost me about £1-1 shilling.

We had decided to have the reception in the *Windmill* pub. I did not have to pay for the back room, ancient Lily said I could have it as a wedding present and Dad said he would pay for my buffet food, good old Dad. The woman who used to serve behind the bar there, also used to work at the *Norwood Rooms* , she got Dad a cut-price buffet, so that worked out good for him.

The next task was to find us somewhere to live; we went on the council waiting list. Then Richard, who Brian worked with, told us that down the road from Castle Hill, on King Street, there was a second-hand shop and they were advertising for someone to live in the flat above the shop. it was opposite *The Lad's Club*.

We went to look at the place and it was actually a maisonette, it had an alleyway, which had a locked gate to stop prostitutes using the back of the yard, as I'm afraid King Street was a well-known kerb-crawler area.

The door went straight up, they were very steep, just like terrace house stairs and there were more than thirteen steps. Then there was another door leading into the kitchen, quite small with a little cooker in it, no fridge but I wasn't used to a fridge anyhow, not like Brian. It had a bath partitioned off and a door leading off to the toilet. Then it went through the kitchen door and on the right were the stairs, then on to the lounge, which had two windows in it, and what looked like an old utility suite, light and airy and a cupboard under the stairs.

Up the stairs was a corridor and on the left was a normal front bedroom with two windows with a double bed in it.

On the other side was a really big bedroom with two double beds and two big wardrobes in. The place would come partly furnished, which was good for us, as we had no money for furniture. We said we would take it, it cost five pounds a week, which was my wages taken care off for the time being. Brian would have to take care of all the rest of the bills, but I would not have to bus or anything as it was just down the hill from Ber Street and it was just around the corner from Panks where Brian worked, so Brian would need no travel money.

There was no heating in the place at all.

Brian's mum made us curtains, blue for the lounge and lilac in the bedroom. Brian's dad painted and papered, so it would be ready for us to move in to as soon as the wedding was over, so at least we would start married life on our own.

Next, I had to get something to wear, Brian said that he had got a suit he had worn for his sister's wedding and it still fitted. I bought my dress from *Peter Robinson's*, which is now called *Top Shop* on Gentleman's Walk. It was a long, pale pink, dress with a tiny pleated bodice, which had a tiny flounce around the waist and it had long sleeves with a flounce on the cuffs, all over, it had tiny darker pink rosebuds, and to finish it off I got a pale pink sunhat with a wide brim.

I bought white platform shoes from *Dolcis*, again on the Walk, all the good shops were around Gentleman's Walk and up St. Stephens, that was me sorted, except for the borrowed and blue.

Brian's 'Meatloaf' friend said he would use his car and chauffer us about on the day as a wedding present, so that was nice.

Peter, the landscape gardener, was going to be best man; I do not know why Paul wasn't, as he was really Brian's best friend at the time.

I was being sick at 11 o'clock every morning on the dot at work and had gone off sweet tea, I now only drunk it with one sugar after that

I told the girls at work the date, and the pay office, but was afraid I could not ask them to the wedding, as there would not be room as I had a big family. They said they would stand outside the

Registry Office, which was very nice, mind you I think a few changed their minds when they knew it was at 10 o'clock in the morning. Lyndsy was a very arty-crafty person and made me a beautiful white horseshoe that I could carry and she had a long blue petticoat that I could wear, so that was the borrowed and blue, how kind some people could be.

Pam asked me if I had an engagement ring, but how could I have when it did not quite get to that, she gave me a lovely blue dress ring and I had that to wear after I had put my wedding band on. Wasn't she kind? Pam was still with the boy that she had met at work and of course, as she was my best friend at the time, she had been invited.

We had not got anywhere to go for a honeymoon, we had thought that we could have gone to his parent's caravan at Hemsby, but it already had a booking for it and could not be changed, but we could have it in September.

The week before I got married, the girls had collected money for my wedding present and I went down to Jarrold's on the corner of Exchange Street and Little London Street, which was just off Gentleman's Walk.

I purchased a very good named cutlery set, I still have some knives and forks remaining. I also bought a wooden standard lamp with a blue shade and the girls were pleased with what I had bought. Yvonne helped me take it all to the King Street residence and it was the first time that she had seen where I was going to live and she liked it.

Brian and I had not had a lot of 'us' time since finding out I was pregnant and I think that we had spent one night in the place before the wedding. We decided to have our respective hen/stag night on the Thursday before the wedding. Mine was a complete washout, not much enthusiasm for it. Yvonne, Peter's girlfriend Gloria (the other Yvonne).Pam, none of my sisters, we went to a few pubs but the girls just wanted to see the boys so I did not drink a lot (yes we did drink in those days when we were pregnant, never thought much about it) and it finished early. Brian had given Peter the key to our place so he and his au pair could stay the night together, not in our bed but in the other room. I went down there on the Friday as I had finished work on the Thursday for a week's holiday after the wedding and Peter's girlfriend had left dirty cotton buds and cotton wool she had been using on the draining board. Why could she have not put them in the bin? I was not best pleased as I had to clear it up.

I had taken most of my clothes and accessories up to the maisonette in two runs on the bus.

I went shopping in the dinnertime, when Brian had his lunch, we went to Tesco's on St. Giles, which was ten minutes' walk from King Street and we spent £1-10 shillings on groceries and that was including the meat for the week.

Brian and I spent a little time there to ourselves on that Friday night and then we walked home to our separate houses for the eve of our wedding and I was getting very nervous .Pam came around to my house that evening with her hair dryer, as I would not have time to wash it in the morning. We laid all my clothes and bits and pieces out and I had a posy in water with a few buttonholes which Dad had got from the florists and paid for them himself.

My dad was so supportive to me, although he did not always agree with everything that I had done.

Saturday the third had arrived, and my car with driver turned up and he had even put a suit and had a cap on, wasn't that a lovely gesture? Dad and I went to get into the car and people were out in the street and, Alan the ex, actually said good luck to me but I think it was said with tongue in cheek. We got in the car and on the way my dad was holding my hand and he said, "You don't have to get married if you don't want to, you've got a home here with me."

"Oh Dad, I'm alright and I don't want my baby out of wedlock," and I believed at that time I was in love with Brian.

"So be it then."

I have often thought of that conversation later on in life, but at that time, I could only think that I would rather do housework in my own place then have to stay at home and do it for the rest of the family.

Dad and I got to the registry office and the car was allowed to wait outside at that time. I saw that most of the family who were coming had arrived and we went into the waiting room and Brian wasn't there. I thought it was the bride who was supposed to be late. Everyone was thinking he wasn't coming but he suddenly arrived all sheepish and he said, "We were going round and round trying to park Peter's van, as that is what they came in, but all was well.

We traipsed into the wedding room and sat down and then I heard my nan say, "Take that bloody hat off we can't see your face."

Nan used to talk quite loud at times but I think it was because she was going a bit deaf and did not realise how loud she was, but I could have died with embarrassment. I turned round gave her a smile and put my finger to my lips and then she went quiet. I did the usual thing and muddled the words up as I was so nervous, everyone just laughed so that released some of the tension on both sides and Brian was grinning at me.

The ceremony and the signing of the certificate done, we went out hand in hand and the first thing I saw was a few of the girls waiting outside to see me, so I gave them a wave. We had a bit of confetti thrown over us. Brian's mum and his sister Carol had cameras so we did have a few pictures.

Then 'Meatloaf' drove us on to the reception, it was a bit early for the pub to open but Lily did and we all had a drink of sherry,

I liked sherry, still do.

The buffet looked lovely, Dad had done me proud and Brian and his parents had put £25 pound behind the bar, which was more than enough in those days.

Then the time came for the best-man to read cards and telegrams out. I had a telegram from David, who was in Germany at the time and could not get leave, one from Rosemary, who was not there, and of course loads of cards. Then, lo and behold, talk about taking my limelight away, Pam's boyfriend made an announcement, hoped I did not mind, that he and Pam had just got engaged, everyone clapped and smiled.

Then someone said, "Hope you've got something to watch tonight as I doubt if you're staying here all night."

"I said, "Blast, that's one thing that I forgot, a television license."

So I collected my purse and ran up the road in all my gear (got several toots on the way), to the post office but it had just shut, so that weekend night we watched telly without one, it was only a black and white one.

Back at the reception, Brian's dad must have been drunk because the next thing I know, he had tipped a glass of beer over my dress. Apologies and napkins later, I went into the toilets to clean up before it stained too much, I had not brought anything to change into as my dress was not like a full bridal gown and I had thought I would be alright.

More apologies as I came out of the toilet, "Accidents happen," I said and then I think Brian's mum took him home.

I then did the rounds and decided I wanted to go home as well and 'Meatloaf' said, "I'll take you home as I have a party somewhere else to go to."

Brian had the big gate keys in his pocket and so off we went to King Street and he said, "I'll pick you up and carry you over the first threshold but don't expect me to carry you up those bloody stairs."

So up the stairs to start married life.

BUT THAT'S ANOTHER STORY.